LONGMAN PRACTICE NOTES

COUNTY COURT PROCEDURE

1ST EDITION

Stephen M Gerlis

Registrar
Brentford County Court

SERIES EDITOR:

CM Brand, Solicitor and Lecturer in Law
University of Liverpool

LONGMAN

© Longman Group UK Ltd 1989

ISBN 085121 5270

Published by
Longman Law, Tax and Finance
Longman Group UK Ltd
21–27 Lamb's Conduit Street
London WC1N 3NJ

Associated Offices
Australia, Hong Kong, Malaysia, Singapore, USA

A CIP catalogue record for this book is available from the British Library

Printed in Great Britain by
Biddles Ltd, Guildford, Surrey

CONTENTS

ACKNOWLEDGMENTS

With grateful thanks to David Price, the Conlon family, Elizabeth Bonham, John Ward and the staff at Brentford County Court for their assistance.

CHAPTER 1

BASIC INFORMATION

1.1 Introduction

1.1.1 The courts Ninety per cent of all litigation in England and Wales is now dealt with by the county courts which are locally based and, with exception in certain cases, have jurisdiction dictated by the local area that they cover. The general jurisdiction of the courts is provided by the County Courts Act 1984 with procedure being regulated by the County Court Rules 1981 as amended. County courts also have special jurisdiction conferred on them by various statutes eg Rent & Housing Acts, Landlord & Tenant Acts, Consumer Credit Act 1974 etc. Some county courts are also district registries of the High Court. Similarly, some county courts have jurisdiction to deal with divorce, bankruptcy or admiralty matters. This book only covers the civil jurisdiction which is common to all county courts. The High Court also has wide power to refer cases to the county court (see 8.3).

1.1.2 Court officials Full-time circuit judges preside over the county courts. They are supplemented by deputy judges, recorders and assistant recorders.

Registrars are full-time assistant judges who deal with the bulk of the interlocutory (see Chapter 6) and enforcement (see Chapter 13) work, arbitrations and small claims (see Chapter 9), undefended mortgage and housing possession and consumer credit cases and have limited open court jurisdiction up to £1,000 (see 10.1.1). They are supplemented by part-time deputy registrars.

The chief clerk is responsible for the administration of the court and delegation and performance of certain non-judicial functions including eg conducting oral examinations (see 13.2).

1.1.3 References Common abbreviations throughout the text include:

- County Courts Act 1984 — 'CCA 1984'
- County Court Rules 1981 — referred to by Order and Rule number eg 'Ord 9, r 14'
- County Court (Amendment) Rules 1989 — 'CC (Amendment) Rules 1989'

- Rules of the Supreme Court—'RSC'

In addition, prescribed official forms are described according to their number in the *County Court Practice* (see below) and each has the prefix 'N' eg N 439. Some forms are available from courts offices free of charge or from law stationers.

All the relevant statutes, rules and orders can be found in the *County Court Practice* which is published annually and is popularly known as the 'Green Book'. Reference is also made to the '*County Court Practice Handbook*' (Ninth Edition) by Robert Blackford, published by Longman.

1.1.4 Know your court In many respects practice varies from court to court. It is important, therefore, to have a knowledge of your local courts and their practice and procedure in matters such as pretrial directions, amounts allowed on taxation, manner of listing and hearing cases, etc.

1.1.5 Civil justice review At the time of writing legislation is proposed to greatly increase the importance and jurisdiction of the county courts, leaving the High Court to concentrate on matters of special significance or complexity.

1.2 Jurisdiction

1.2.1 Contract and tort Where sums of up to £5,000 are involved a number of points should be noted:

(1) Actions to recover sums due under any enactment where the High Court does not have exclusive jurisdiction are included.

(2) Also included are claims under Torts (Interference with Goods) Act 1977.

(3) Libel and slander are not included (CCA 1984, s 15(2) (*c*)) except by agreement under CCA 1984, s 18, or as a counterclaim (CCA 1984, s 43).

(4) Interest claimed pursuant to CCA 1984, s 69 is excluded when calculating the limit but not interest payable under contract or any other statute.

1.2.2 Recovery of land Where net annual value for rating ('nav') does not exceed £1,000, it should be noted that:

(1) This includes actions for forfeiture of leases for non-payment of

rent (CCA 1984, s 138) or for breach of some other covenant (Law of Property Act 1925, s 146).

(2) The same limit applies to actions concerning title to land.

(3) Where land is not separately rated it will be taken to have a 'nav' not exceeding that of the hereditament of which it forms part and, subject to this, is deemed to have a 'nav' equal to its value by the year. Even if the 'nav' exceeds the above limits the parties can consent to the county court having jurisdiction.

(4) Under the Rent Act 1977 and Housing Acts 1985 and 1988:

• the court has jurisdiction even if the amount claimed is over the county court limit subject to the 'nav' limits below; and

• in Rent Act tenancies the 'nav' must not exceed £1,500 in Greater London or £1,000 elsewhere.

• a 'secure' tenancy under the Housing Act 1985 is generally one within the public sector so the 'nav' limits do not apply; and

• an 'assured' tenancy under the Housing Act 1988 must not have a 'nav' exceeding £1,500 in Greater London and £750 elsewhere.

1.2.3 Mortgage possession actions   The county court will have jurisdiction even if the amount claimed is more than £5,000 provided the property is within the 'nav' limits (£1,500 'nav' in Greater London and £1,000 'nav' elsewhere).

There is no financial limit on the county courts' jurisdiction in cases of mortgages secured on land by way of a regulated agreement under s 189(i) of the Consumer Credit Act 1974.

1.2.4 Equity proceedings (CCA 1984, s 23)   The limit for equity proceedings in the county court is £30,000 being the value of:

(1) The net estate of the deceased in an administration.

(2) A trust where the question of its execution, substance or variation under the Variation of Trusts Act 1958 is at issue.

(3) The amount owed in an action for foreclosure or redemption of a mortgage or to enforce any charge or lien.

(4) The purchase money in an action for specific performance, rectification, delivery up or cancellation of any agreement for sale, or the value of property in the case of a lease.

(5) The property of an infant in an action for maintenance or advancement.

(6) The assets in an action for dissolution or winding up of a partnership.

(7) The fund involved in an action for relief from fraud or mistake.

Under s 25 of the CCA 1984 the county court has equity jurisdiction under the following enactments, if the parties agree, notwithstanding any limit on jurisdiction contained in these enactments:

- Settled Land Act 1925
- Trustee Act 1925
- Law of Property Act 1925
- Land Charges Act 1925
- Administration of Estates Act 1925
- Leasehold Property (Repairs) Act 1938

The court also has jurisdiction to entertain applications for relief from forfeiture of leases under s 146 of the Law of Property Act 1925 where 'nav' does not exceed £1,000.

1.2.5 Probate and counterclaims In a probate action the county court has jurisdiction only where the net estate does not exceed £30,000. In contrast, there is no limit on counterclaims in the county court.

1.2.6 Declarations and injunctions In the county court declarations and injunctions are either:

- ancillary to a claim within jurisdiction; or
- under specific enactment eg Domestic Violence and Matrimonial Proceedings Act 1976, Part II of the Landlord and Tenant Act 1954, the Race Relations Act 1976, and the Sex Discrimination Act 1975; or
- in relation to land where 'nav' is within the court's jurisdiction.

1.2.7 Specific delivery of goods and replevin In the county court there is a £5,000 limit on the specific delivery of goods but for replevin (the redelivery of wrongfully seized goods) there is no limit.

1.2.8 Hire purchase, conditional sale agreements and the Consumer Credit Act 1974 For agreements on or before 18 May 1985 there is jurisdiction for the recovery of goods where:

- the hirer or buyer is not a corporate body;
- the hire or purchase price does not exceed £7,500; and
- one-third of price has been paid.

For agreements after 18 May 1985 the jurisdiction for the recovery of goods is the same as above but the limit is £15,000.

1.2.9   By consent   The jurisdiction can be exceeded if both parties agree to the county court dealing with the matter. This applies to actions which would otherwise be dealt with by the Queens Bench Division and equity proceedings otherwise limited by statute other than under the Variation of Trusts Act 1958.

1.2.10   Admiralty   County courts have jurisdiction in some instances. For a specific listing see the *County Court Practice* (1989), p 952.

1.2.11   Special statutory jurisdiction   The county court also had jurisdiction bestowed upon it by various statutes of which some of the more significant are discussed in Chapter 16. For a comprehensive list see the *County Court Practice* (1989), p 948.

1.2.12   Wrong jurisdiction   The court may:

• retain the matter if the parties consent;
• transfer it to the High Court if it is above county court jurisdiction;
• strike out proceedings; or
• transfer to the appropriate county court if the venue was wrong (see 2.1).

CHAPTER 2

COMMENCEMENT OF PROCEEDINGS

2.1 Venue

2.1.1 Actions Actions to recover money, fixed date actions, admiralty and rent actions are commenced either in the court district where the defendant resides or carries on business or in which the cause of action wholly or partly arises. 'Carries on business' means the trading address of a defendant not the place of employment of an individual defendant (unless he is self-employed).

2.1.2 Income tax proceedings In income tax proceedings the cause of action arises at the office of the collector of taxes making the demand.

2.1.3 Assignee The assignee sues in the court the assignor would have had to use.

2.1.4 Tort Where a defendant does not reside or carry on business in England and Wales, the court for the district where the plaintiff resides or carries on business is the appropriate venue for tort cases.

2.1.5 Hire purchase, conditional scale agreements and the Consumer Credit Act 1974 Actions concerning hire purchase or conditional sale agreements where delivery of goods is not claimed or contracts for the sale or hire of goods under which sale or rental price is payable by more than one instalment, whether or not delivery of goods are claimed, must be commenced only in the court for the district in which any defendant resides or carries on business either at the commencement of the action or when the contract was made. However, actions under the Hire Purchase Act 1965 for delivery of goods or where the agreement was made on or after 19 May 1965 are commenced in the court for the district in which any defendant resides or carries on business or did so at the time of the last payment under the contract.

2.1.6 Actions against the crown These are taken in the district in which the cause of action wholly or partly arose.

2.1.7   Recovery of land   The recovery of land by foreclosure or redemption of mortgage, enforcing charge (other than charging order) or lien on land, must be taken in the court of the district where the land is situated.

2.1.8   Enforcing charging order on land   If pursuant to a court order, this must be done in the district of the court that made the order. Otherwise, it is taken in the district of the defendant's residence or business or, if none, in the district of the plaintiff's residence or business.

2.1.9   Settled Land 1925, Trustee Act 1925 or administration of deceased's estate   Proceedings are commenced in the court which the plaintiff regards as most convenient.

2.1.10   Dissolution or winding up of a partnership   Proceedings are commenced in the district in which the partnership or business was or is carried on.

2.1.11   Originating applications and petitions   These may be subject to specific enactments or rules or, failing this, may be commenced in the district in which the respondent lives or carries on business or in which the subject matter of the application is situated, or, if no respondent is named, the district where the applicant or petitioner resides or carries on business.

2.1.12   Appeals to county courts   These are commenced in the court for the district in which the order appealed against was made.

2.1.13   Payment into court   This is made to a court in whose district the person making the payment resides.

2.2   Parties

2.2.1   Limited companies   The address for service given in the summons must be that of the registered office of the company or its place of business (r 3 of the CC (Amendment) Rules 1989 amending Ord 7, r 14).

2.2.2   The Crown   The title of the appropriate department should be precisely stated on the document (see *County Court Practice* (1989), pp 1210–11).

2.2.3 Partners and business names Any one of two or more partners may sue or be sued in the name of the firm. (Ord 5, r 9(1)). If the name of the business is not that of the person being sued the words 'trading as AB' should follow that person's name or the business name used followed by 'a trading name'. Where partners sue or are sued in a firm's name the words 'suing as a firm' or 'sued as a firm' as appropriate should appear after the name. On written demand the partners can be compelled to reveal the names and addresses of all the partners (Ord 5, r 9(2)).

2.2.4 Persons under a disability This includes minors or mental patients:

- Such persons can only bring or defend proceedings through a next friend or guardian ad litem (Ord 10, r 1(1), (2)), save that a minor can sue for wages (CCA 1984, s 47).
- The next friend of a plaintiff or applicant must file an undertaking (N 235) to be responsible for costs (Ord 10, r 2(*a*)).
- If there is no 'next friend' of the plaintiff or applicant the court may appoint one (Ord 10, r 3).
- Where the person under a disability is a defendant or respondent a guardian ad litem may be appointed on application by the plaintiff or applicant (Ord 10, r 6) but the guardian has no personal liability for costs unless they are negligent or in cases of misconduct.
- Unless the court otherwise directs monies recovered by a person under a disability are invested by the court, other than claims for wages by minors (Ord 10, r 11).
- For further details concerning persons under a disability see the *County Court Practice Handbook*, p 24.

2.2.5 Bankruptcy If the plaintiff becomes bankrupt the action can only continue if the trustee elects to do so and gives security for costs. If the defendant becomes bankrupt or, if a company is wound up, the plaintiff in a money claim ought to consider whether it is worthwhile continuing with the proceedings or submitting a proof of debt. A trustee in bankruptcy should sue or be sued as 'trustee of the estate of AB a bankrupt'.

2.2.6 Death of a party When this occurs the personal representatives should take over the action if the action survives (Ord 5, rr 7 and 12).

2.2.7 Common mistakes There are a number of common mistakes which are to be avoided such as:

- Suing an insurance company instead of the insured.
- Suing a director of a company for a debt incurred only by the company.
- Suing an agent acting for a disclosed principal (eg managing agents instead of landlords).
- Forgetting to add the employer as a defendant to an action against an employee where vicarious liability is involved.
- Suing a firm when it is in fact a company and vice versa. It is a good idea to check very carefully exactly who you are suing. Invoices, statements or even a company search may prove helpful. Also note that sometimes a company trades as a firm but never vice versa. In such a case they should be described as 'AB Company Limited trading as CD a firm'.
- Giving a 'C/O' address for a party without leave of the court.
- Not giving the full names of the plaintiff.

2.3 Types of action

2.3.1 Actions These include:

- Fixed date ie where relief other than money is claimed (see Diagram A on p 10).
- Rent ie for arrears only.
- Default ie for payment of money only (see Diagram B on p 11).
- Admiralty (see *County Court Practice* (1989), p 952).

2.3.2 Matters These include:

- Originating applications ie where no other form of proceeding is specified.
- Summary proceedings for recovery of land.
- Petitions.
- Appeals to the county court.
- Other proceedings specifically provided for.

2.4 Requirements

2.4.1 Actions For fixed date, rent and default actions (Ord 3, r 3) there are a number of requirements. These include:

(1) The appropriate form of request (N 201–204).

(2) Particulars of claim with a copy for each defendant. It is important to note that in default actions it is possible to have a combined form of request and particulars of claim (N 202).

Diagram A: Steps in a Fixed Date Summons

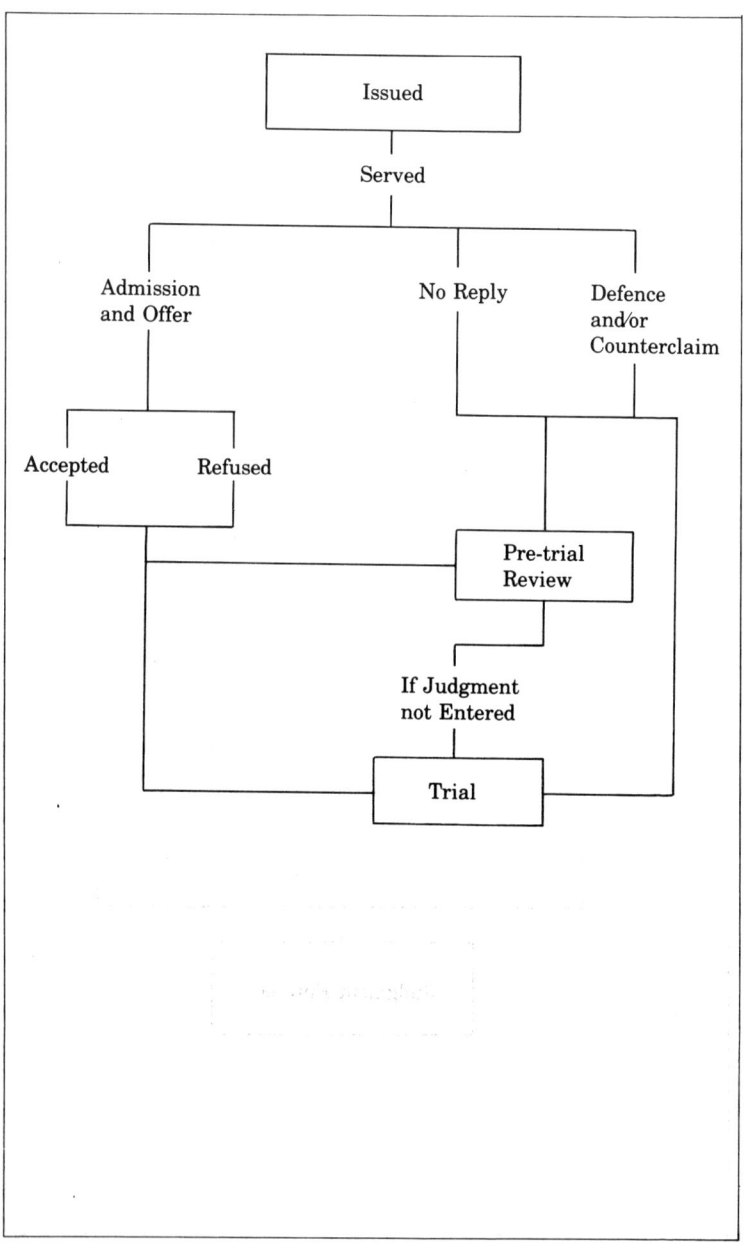

Diagram B: Steps in a Default Summons

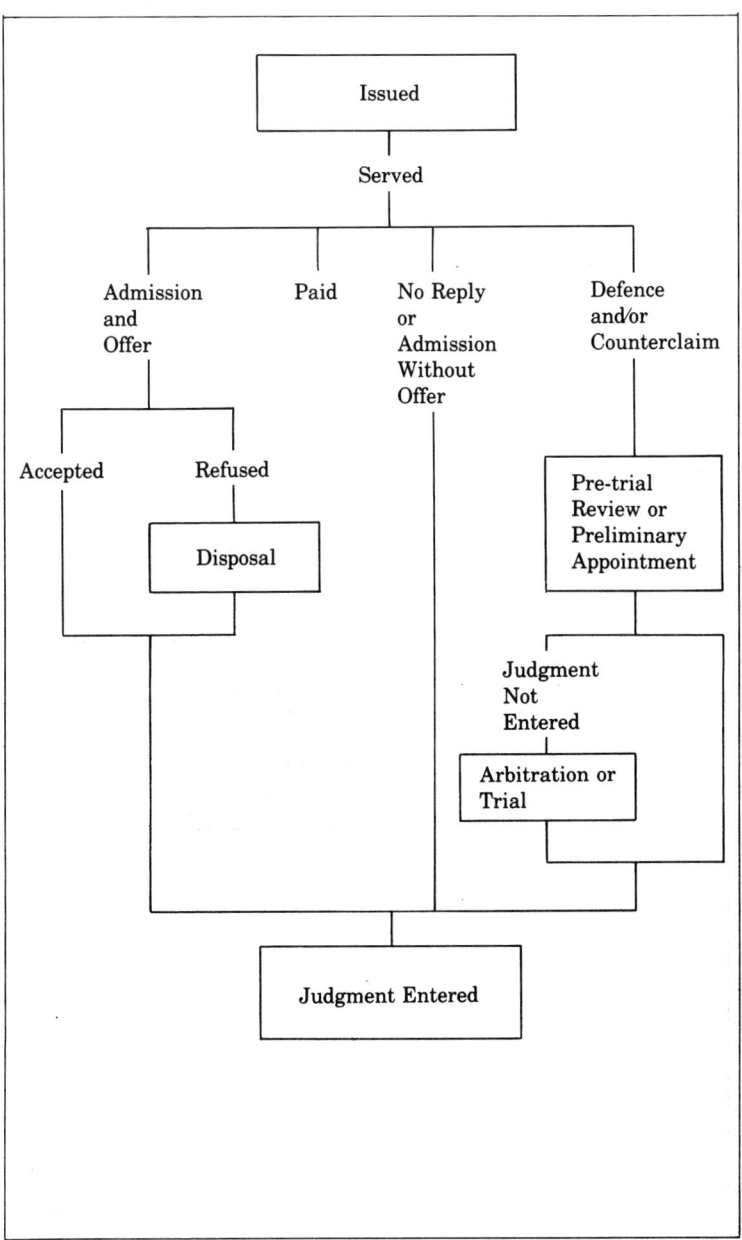

(3) Plaint fee (See Table of Fees) (and bailiff's fee if appropriate) by cash, postal order, bankers draft, and (subject to clearance and chief clerk's consent) cheques made payable to HM Paymaster-General and crossed. Solicitors cheques are usually accepted.

(4) Self-addressed envelope, if issued by post.

(5) Where the plaintiff is under a disability an undertaking by next friend (see 2.2.4).

(6) Civil aid certificate, if any, and notice of certificate for service on defendant.

Note: Appropriate amounts for court and solicitors fees should be entered on the request for the summons (see Appendix 2). When the proceedings are issued a plaint note is supplied to the plaintiff which, in the case of a fixed date summons, shows the return day. There will also be a plaint number. It is very important to note this and refer to it in all future communications with the court because the court files matters according to the plaint number and not the names of the parties.

2.4.2 Originating applications (Ord 3, r 4) The requirements are as follows:

• request for issue (no prescribed form). Parties should be described as 'Applicant' and 'Respondent'.
• Originating application with a copy for each respondent.
• Appropriate fee for issue (see Table of Fees).
• Self-addressed envelope, if issued by post.
• If applicant is under a disability an undertaking by next friend as to costs (see 2.2.4).
• Civil aid certificate, if any, and notice of certificate for service on respondent.

Note: A plaint note is issued by the court and will state a date either for a hearing or a pre-trial review.

2.4.3 Summary proceedings for recovery of land (Ord 24, rr 1–7) This includes actions against eg squatters, trespassers and unlawful subtenants. Requirements include:

• An originating application (N 312) with a copy for each named respondent and two further copies.
• An affidavit in support with copies as above.
• Fee for issue (see Table of Fees) and, if appropriate, for bailiff's service.

- Self-addressed envelope, if issued by post.
- If the applicant does not know the names of some or all of the respondents they may be described in the pleadings as 'persons unknown'.
- The court will issue a plaint note which will contain a hearing date.

2.4.4   Petitions (Ord 3, r 5)   Requirements are as for originating applications above save that 'petitioner' is substituted for 'applicant'.

2.4.5   Appeals (Ord 3, r 6)   The requirements for appeals in the county court are as follows:

- Request for entry of appeal (N 209) with a copy for each respondent.
- Copy of the decision appealed against.
- Where required by appropriate enactment, a copy of any notice of intention to appeal. In every other case the grounds for appeal must be included in the request (N 209).
- Fee for issue (see Table of Fees) and, if appropriate, for bailiffs service.
- Self addressed envelope, if issued by post.

2.5 Particulars of claim

2.5.1   Joinder of causes and parties (Ord 5, rr 1–4)   The plaintiff may claim relief for more than one cause of action in the same action where the parties' capacities are the same or where they all relate to the administration of the same estate. Similarly, two or more persons may be joined together as parties in an action arising out of the same transactions.

2.5.2   Generally   The particulars must be signed either by the plaintiff or solicitors acting on his/her behalf who must also state that they will accept service of proceedings on the plaintiffs behalf and giving their address for service. Counsel's name should appear on any particulars settled by him/her and in debt claims the nature of the consideration should be shown eg 'for services rendered' or 'for goods sold and delivered'.

The date of any invoice should be stated and in an accident claim sufficient details of the date, place and alleged negligence of the defendant in relation to the accident should be given.

A sufficient cause of action must be shown. Examples of inadequate particulars are: (in an action against dry cleaners) 'lost dress'; (in an action for breach of contract) 'damages for breach of contract'; (in a road traffic case) 'repairs to damaged vehicle'. Any interest claimed either under contract or pursuant to s 69 of the County Courts Act 1984 must be specifically pleaded showing both the calculation for interest up to the date of issue of proceedings and the daily rate claimed thereafter (see 11.3.7). An application to amend the particulars to claim interest at a later stage may not automatically be granted. The present court rate is 15 per cent per annum.

2.5.3 Recovery of Land (Ord 6, r 3) Particulars must contain:

- A full description of the land.
- 'Nav' (see 1.2.2) or, where not separately rated, the 'nav' of the hereditament of which it forms part of the value of the land by the year.
- The amount of the rent, if any.
- Grounds for possession.
- In proceedings for re-entry or forfeiture for non-payment of rent (CCA 1984, s 138) the daily rate for rent in arrear or mesne profits.
- In proceedings for forfeiture the names and addresses of any mortgagee or underlessee entitled to claim relief.

For injunctions and declarations relating to land where there is no other claim a full description of the land and 'nav' must be given.

2.5.4 Mortgage actions (Ord 6, r 5) Particulars must state:

- The date of the mortgage.
- The amount of advance, instalments required, amount of interest, amount of arrears, and balance due.
- Any proceedings the plaintiff has taken in respect of monies secured and, if money only is claimed, whether the plaintiff already has possession.
- Where possession is claimed, if it is of a dwelling house within the meaning of Part IV of the Administration of Justice Act 1970.
- Where a dwelling house, if there is any person who ought to be served with notice of proceedings under s 8(3) of the Matrimonial Homes Act 1983 giving full details.

2.5.5 Hire purchase actions For agreements dated on or after 19 May 1985 (Ord 6, r 6) and where a plaintiff claims delivery of goods let under a hire purchase agreement to a person other than a body corporate, particulars shall state in order:

- Date of agreement and parties to it and number of agreement or sufficient particulars to enable debtor to identify it.
- Details of any transfer of creditor.

- Whether there is a regulated agreement and, if not, the reason why.
- Place where agreement signed by hirer.
- Goods claimed.
- Total price.
- Paid up sum.
- Unpaid balance.
- Whether default notice under s 76(1) or s 98(1) of the Consumer Credit Act 1974 has been served on the debtor and, if so, the date and manner of service.
- Date when right to demand delivery accrued.
- Amount (if any) claimed as alternative to delivery.
- Amount (if any) claimed in addition to delivery or claim as an alternative to delivery.

It is important to note that where delivery is not claimed, particulars are as in the first seven points above together with details of arrears of instalments (if any) and any other claim with details of how it arises. For particulars where agreements pre-date 19 May 1985 see the *County Court Practice Handbook*, p 43.

2.5.6   Actions against the Crown   The particulars must identify the government officers and departments involved and details of the circumstances under which the liability of the Crown is alleged to have arisen.

CHAPTER 3

LIMITATION PERIODS AND COMPUTATION OF TIME

3.1 Limitation periods

The limitation periods for various types of actions are as follows:

(1) Land—12 years from the date the right of action accrued.
(2) Contract and tort—Six years from the date the cause of action accrued.
(3) Personal injury—Three years from the date the cause of action accured or (if later) the date of knowledge of injury.
(4) Latent damage—Three years from the date the right of action accrued and the plaintiff had knowledge of material facts but in any event not later than 15 years from the date the act or omission causing damage occurred.
(5) Fraud, concealment or mistake—Time runs from discovery.
(6) Contribution actions—Two years from the date the right to contribution accrued.

3.2 Computation of time

The computation of time (Ord 1, r 9) is calculated so that 'At least 56 days before date of trial' means that time runs from the date the act is done to the day immediately before trial. Similarly, 'within 14 days from todays date' means that time runs from the day after the order is made.

Where the period for compliance is three days or less, the date on which the court is closed (eg weekends, bank holidays) is excluded. However, if the date for compliance expires on the day the court is closed, the next available day applies.

It should be noted that an order requiring an act to be done (other than payment of money) must specify the time within which it is to be done (Ord 22, r 3) stating the length of time involved and the date from which time runs.

CHAPTER 4

SERVICE

4.1 Generally (Order 7)

4.1.1 Service by post Unless personal service is requested, summonses are initially served by the court by first class post. Where service is by post it is deemed to have been effected at the time of usual delivery. However, the court will confirm the service of a summons by post giving the date service is deemed to have been effected (usually seven days after posting).

4.1.2 Personal service Personal service may be by:

- Court bailiff.
- Court official (if at court)
- Party to proceedings, agent or solicitor (affidavit of service necessary (N 215)).

If, however, the bailiff has been unable to serve then a notice of non-service (N 216) will be given.

4.1.3 Limitations on service Fixed date summonses, originating applications, petitions or appeals should be served at least 21 days before the return date unless leave is granted. Service must be effected within one year from the date of issue unless the court grants leave to extend the time on an ex parte application by letter. There is no service on Sunday, Christmas or Good Friday except in a case of urgency with leave or Admiralty action (Ord 7, r 3).

4.1.4 Substituted service Under Ord 7, r 8 a party may make an application for substituted service ex parte upon an affidavit showing grounds. In addition, the type of substituted service should be suggested in the affidavit. If by advertisement, a draft should be submitted to the registrar to settle.

4.2 Service of summons

4.2.1 Recipient in person Unless service is by actual delivery to the person, service is effected in the first instance by delivery or first class post to the address given for service which may be a residence or business or the last known residence or business.

4.2.2   Service on solicitor   Service is deemed to have been effected on the date of the certificate by delivery of the document at, or sending it by first class post to the solicitor's address for service, or a numbered document exchange box. A copy of any originating process so served must be endorsed by the solicitor and returned to the server (including the court).

4.2.3   The Crown   Service is effected by delivery or post on the person authorised to receive service for that particular department (usually on acting solicitor) (see the list of authorised government departments and their solicitors in the *County Court Practice*).

4.2.4   Minors and mental patients   If a defendant is a minor, service is effected on a parent or guardian or, if none, the person with whom s/he resides or in whose care s/he is. If a defendant is a mental patient, summons is served on the person authorised under the Mental Health Act 1983, pt VII, or the person with whom s/he resides or in whose care s/he is.

4.2.5   Partners   Where partners are sued in the name of their firm, service is effected by first class post to the place of business, unless personal service on a particular partner is requested by the plaintiff. If service is by bailiff, (after non-service by post) delivery is made to the business address and served on the person appearing to have control or management (usually a partner) and not on a receptionist, office junior, secretary, tea lady or the like (Ord 7, r 13).

4.2.6   Limited companies   Service is effected on limited companies by leaving the summons at, or sending it by post to the registered office or place of business (Ord 7, r 14 as amended by the CC (Amendment) Rules 1989, r 3).

4.2.7   Corporations aggregate   Service may be effected on the mayor, chairman or president, chief executive, clerk, treasurer or secretary.

4.2.8   Recovery of land   A service of summons for the recovery of land is effected as above failing which with leave of the court, it can be served on the defendant's spouse, cohabitee, lessee, tenant or representative residing or carrying on business at premises. If there is no occupant, with leave of the court, service can be effected by fixing the summons to a prominent or conspicuous part of the property (see also r 11 of the CC (Amendment) Rules 1989).

In Ord 24 cases (see 2.4.3 above) service must be supplemented by affixing the summons to part of the property or by pushing a sealed envelope containing the summons (addressed to 'the occupiers') through the letterbox.

4.2.9 Originating applications   Under the Landlord and Tenant Act 1954, s 24 a summons must be served within two months of issue unless the period is extended by the court.

4.3   Service out of the jurisdiction (Order 8)

Service of an originating process outside England and Wales is permissable without the leave of the court if a claim is one that the court has the power to hear under the Civil Jurisdiction and Judgments Act 1982 (provided there are no current proceedings in the UK or any other commonwealth country) or if the court is empowered by enactment to hear the matter Ord 8, r 2(2).

Leave is required otherwise and is likely to be granted in those cases where broadly, the defendant is domiciled in, or the subject matter of the action is within the UK. (For a complete list where leave is permissable see Ord 8, r 2(1)). An application for leave must be supported by an affidavit or other evidence (Ord 8, r 6).

CHAPTER 5

PLEADINGS

5.1 Admissions, defences, counterclaims and answers

All these responses must be filed within 14 days of the service of the summons (unless it is an originating application in which case another period is specified), either on a form provided (N 9, N 10 or N 11) or by the solicitors' own form in duplicate (Ord 9, r 2).

The defendant's admission, defence or counterclaim must be signed by the defendant if acting in person or by a solicitor if the defendant is absent and an address for service must be given. If the defendant is under disability then the admission must be signed by a guardian ad litem (see 2.2.4).

An admission is still valid if delivered late but it must be before judgment is entered in a default action (see 5.2) or before the return day in a fixed date action. A copy of the admission, with instructions, is sent by the court to the plaintiff. Where there is an admission with an offer to pay the other party or part admission see Diagram C (opposite).

Where only quantum is in dispute but liability is admitted, the plaintiff may apply for interlocutory judgment with damages to be assessed.

Where a defence or counterclaim is filed before judgment is entered, the court will either fix a date for a pre-trial review (N 233) or, where claim does not exceed £500, a pre-arbitration review (N 18) or, where appropriate, a date for hearing (N 232).

5.1.1 Points to note The following points must be borne in mind:

(1) Whilst a bare denial (eg 'The defendant denies that he is indebted to the plaintiff as alleged or at all') may be sufficient to prevent judgment in default being entered (Ord 9, r 17(*a*)), it is unlikely to be satisfactory to the court on the pre-trial or pre-arbitration review or at the hearing of the matter (see Chapter 7). The defendant must file a full and proper response to the Particulars of Claim (see RSC Ord 18, r 12).

(2) Some courts, on receipt of a defence or counterclaim, may make directions of their own motion, obviating the need for a pre-trial

Diagram C: Disposal

(Ord 9, r 3 as amended by r 4 of the CC (Amendment) Rules 1989)

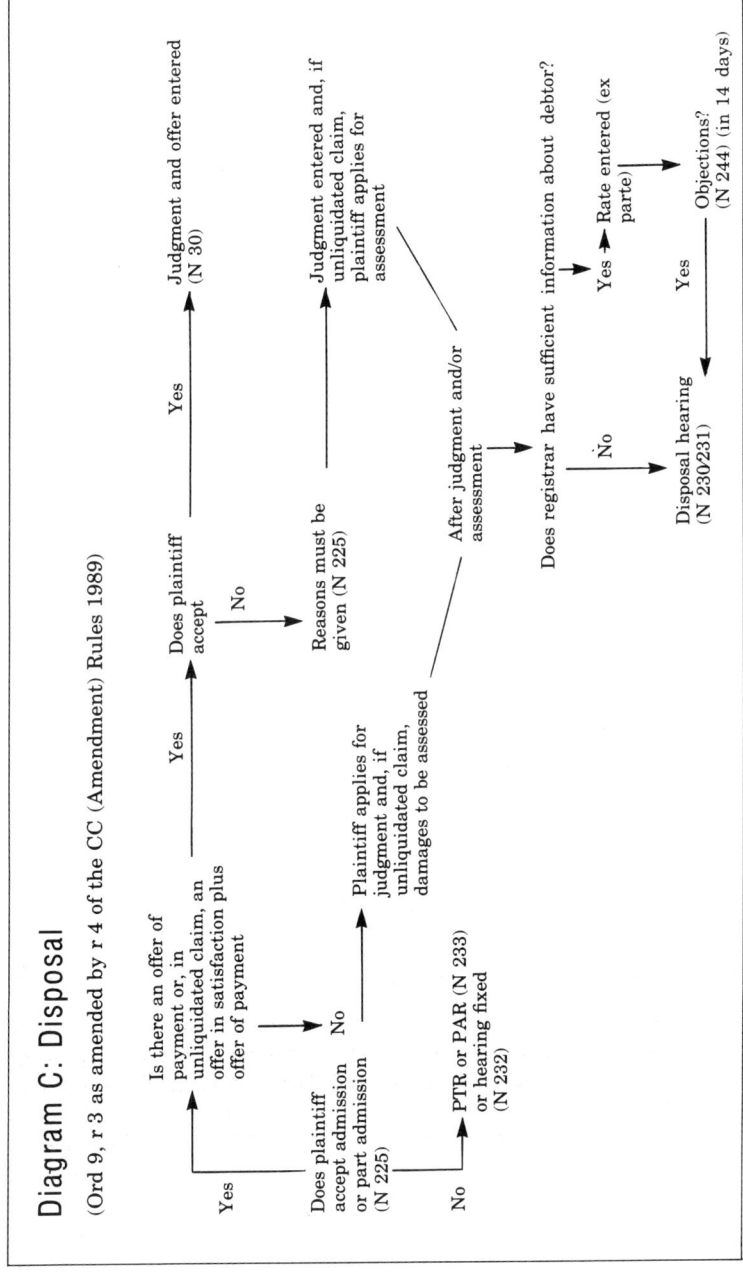

or pre-arbitration review. This is particularly so in road traffic cases.

(3) Where a defence is filed in an action for recovery of land the return date may be utilised as a pre-trial review, if the court thinks it appropriate.

(4) Where 12 months have elapsed since service and no further step has been taken either by the plaintiff (including after an admission) or the defendant, the action is struck out and cannot be revived (Ord 9, r 10). Note also that if no application is made within 12 months of the case being adjourned generally the court may give notice of its intention to strike the matter out if no application to fix a hearing date or adjourn the matter is issued within 14 days (Ord 13, r 3(4)). The application can be made ex parte (Ord 13, r 3 (5) (6) added by r 6 of the CC (Amendment) Rules 1989).

(5) Any documents sent to the court must contain the plaint number.

(6) If the counterclaim exceeds the claim an excess fee is payable.

(7) Answers to originating summonses are only required when specified by the rules or ordered by the court.

(8) Failure to file a defence to a fixed date action prior to the return date may not be fatal but the court will need to be satisfied that there is a prima facie defence and that one will be filed in the near future.

5.1.2 Reply to defence A reply to defence normally accompanies the defence to a counterclaim but otherwise is not essential other than to rebut an allegation of fact in the defence.

5.1.3 Further and better particulars If the defendant is seeking more details a written request should be served on the plaintiff first. If there is no reply, an order of the court should be sought by an application on notice which must be accompanied by details of the further particulars sought. The particulars, when supplied, should incorporate the request (Ord 6, r 7(4)).

5.1.4 Interrogatories Under the provisions of Ord 14, r 11 an application is to be made on notice in Form N 244. This must be accompanied by a copy of the proposed questions when served.

5.1.5 Amendment Pleadings may be amended without leave of the court at any time prior to the pre-trial review date or fixed date hearing (Ord 15, r 2(1) as amended by the CC (Amendment) Rules 1989, r 7). Otherwise an application to amend is on notice and is accompanied by details of the proposed amendments. A clerical error may be corrected by the court at any time and no person can be added as a plaintiff without his/her consent in writing.

5.2 Judgment in default (Order 9, r 6)

Where there is no response filed in default actions or where there is an unqualified admission the plaintiff may apply for judgment in default using form N 14 (or N 214 in claims for unliquidated damages). The appropriate request form should be accompanied by the plaint note and a stamped addressed envelope (if by post).

No judgment in default may be obtained against the Crown or where service is effected outside the UK or inside the UK (on a person domiciled in Scotland, Northern Ireland or a Convention Country) without leave of the court.

Interest, where claimed in the particulars of claim (see 2.5.2), may be given up to the date that judgment is entered, but in the county court it does not run any further. If needed, interim payment of damages can be applied for where the amount involved in proceedings exceeds £500 (Ord 13, r 12).

If an interlocutory judgment has been granted it is up to the plaintiff to apply for an appointment for assessment (N 244) unless the court has already given a date.

CHAPTER 6

INTERLOCUTORY APPLICATIONS

6.1 Applications generally

6.1.1 Basic procedure Under Ord 13, r 1 the following items are required:

- Unless otherwise directed applications must be made on written notice (if not ex parte) using Form N 244 plus a copy for each respondent to the application.
- Although not mandatory, if a time estimate can be given it assists the court.
- Unless otherwise directed, the application will be heard by the registrar in chambers.
- At least two days' notice must be given to the respondent unless the court or the rules state otherwise.
- Appeals to the judge from the registrar must be filed and served within five days of the interlocutory order appealed against (see 14.1.1) unless the judge extends the time.
- Agreed applications may be dealt with by post without a hearing.

6.1.2 Adjournment If the parties consent to an adjournment it may be granted by post, but a reason for the request is usually expected by the court.

An application to restore a matter after being 'adjourned generally' is usually made by a request in writing, with a copy sent to all other parties. Notice of the new hearing is sent by the court, which may vary a hearing date of its own motion.

6.1.3 Summary judgment Application may be made only in default actions and where the claim exceeds £500 and the defendant has delivered a defence to the court. See also 11.2.

6.2 Specific applications

6.2.1 Discovery and inspection Under the provisions of Ord 14, rr 1–10 a party may request another party in writing to give discovery by list (N 265) failing which a court order may be sought.

More usually, however, an order for discovery is sought at a pre-trial review (see Chapter 7 below). Only such discovery as is necessary (Ord 14, r 8) will be ordered and it may be limited (Ord 14, r 1(3)) (eg to bills or estimates for repair in an assessment of damages).

Inspection usually follows after discovery (Ord 14, r 4) and failure to provide inspection can result in an application for an order (Ord 14, r 5).

In arbitration matters some courts dispense with the formality of discovery and inspection and require instead that the parties supply each other with copies of all documents upon which they intend to rely. It is important to note that pre-litigation discovery may be sought in personal injury or death cases (Ord 24, r 7A RSC).

6.2.2   Striking out   Under Ord 13, r 5 grounds are that a claim, defence or counterclaim discloses no reasonable cause of action or defence or is scandalous, frivolous or vexatious or may prejudice, embarrass or delay a fair trial or is otherwise an abuse of process.

An application for dismissal for want of prosecution should be made on principles such as *Birkett* v *James* (1978) AC 297, (1977) 2 A11 ER 801. A striking out order is unlikely to be made unless it can be shown that the defendant has suffered prejudice or a fair trial was impossible (*Department of Transport* v *Chris Smaller (Transport) Ltd*, (1989) *The Independent*, 10 March).

It may be prudent to send some reminders to the other party before seeking to strike them out (see Ord 25 r 25(1)(7) (Note 8) RSC). For failure to comply with a court order (see 11.1.2).

6.2.3   Preserving property   The court has the power to order inspection, preservation and detention of any property involved in proceedings (CCA 1984, s 52(1)).

6.2.4   Interim payment   The applicant must satisfy the court that they are bound to succeed against the respondent (Ord 13, r 12).

6.2.5   Injunctions   Under Ord 13, r 6 application is usually made to a judge. The following are required:

- application for injunction plus copy for service;
- affidavit in support plus copy for service;
- draft order (N 16); and
- fee for bailiff service if required (see Table of Fees).

Where the application is made at the same time as the issue of proceedings then in addition to the above the appropriate documents as set out in 2.4 will also be required. However, where an application is made before proceedings are issued the court will normally require a draft of the proposed particulars of claim and an undertaking to issue proceedings within a very short period.

6.2.6 Consolidation The consolidation of proceedings is appropriate where there are two or more pending actions in the same court and it appears to the court that:

- that there is a common question of fact or law; or
- the claim arises out of the same transaction or series of transactions; or
- there is some other compelling reason to consolidate matters.

The court may either order consolidating the trial of one matter immediately after the other, the trial at the same time or the stay of one matter pending determination of the the other.

6.2.7 Accounts and inquiry The procedure is the same for applying for an injunction (see 6.2.5 above). The registrar may be asked to deal with a reference for inquiry and report (Ord 19, rr 7-9).

6.2.8 Security for costs These may be applied for where:

- a plaintiff (or defendant who counterclaims) ordinarily resides out of the jurisdiction (Ord 13, r 8); or
- a plaintiff limited company is alleged to be unable to pay a successful defendant's costs (Companies Act 1985, s 726).

6.2.9 Discontinuance In a discontinuance of proceedings:

- No application is necessary.
- Notice must be given to the parties (N 279) and to the court.
- Unless the court otherwise orders, the party in receipt of the notice is entitled to claim taxed costs up to the date of receipt of the notice.

A stay of proceedings does not end them unlike a discontinuance or a withdrawal (*Rofasport Management* v *Sport Billy Productions* (1989) *The Independent*, 20 March).

CHAPTER 7

PRE-TRIAL AND PRE-ARBITRATION REVIEW

7.1 Purpose and procedure

Reviews are undertaken prior to proceedings for two reasons: first, if there is no reasonable case in law to be tried, to attempt as far as is possible to dispose of the case, and second, if there *is* a case, to give directions to see that it is properly prepared. The procedure is fully outlined in Ord 17.

7.1.1 Options open to registrar This is dependent on various factors. For an outline see Diagram D (on p 28).

7.1.2 Sample directions As yet there are no agreed standard directions used by every court (see Sample forms 1 on p 70 for an example).

7.1.3 Points to note

(1) Although the rules do not provide for a letter in place of attendance some courts do allow it. Directions are often agreed by both sides who confirm in writing. There is no guarantee that the registrar will make the directions as requested.

(2) Some courts dispense with a review day and give automatic directions.

(3) Any party intending to seek a particular direction on the review should give notice to the court and other parties (Ord 17, rr 1–3).

(4) Whilst the non-attendance of the plaintiff at the pre-trial review may result in the claim being struck out, the non-attendance of the defendant does not mean that the plaintiff can apply for judgment if a valid defence has been filed unless the plaintiff is in a position to prove the claim.

(5) A direction for a 'full and proper defence' ought not to be made without any existing defence being struck out.

(6) To seek leave to amend a pleading or an order for further and

Diagram D: Options Open to Registrar on PTR/PAR

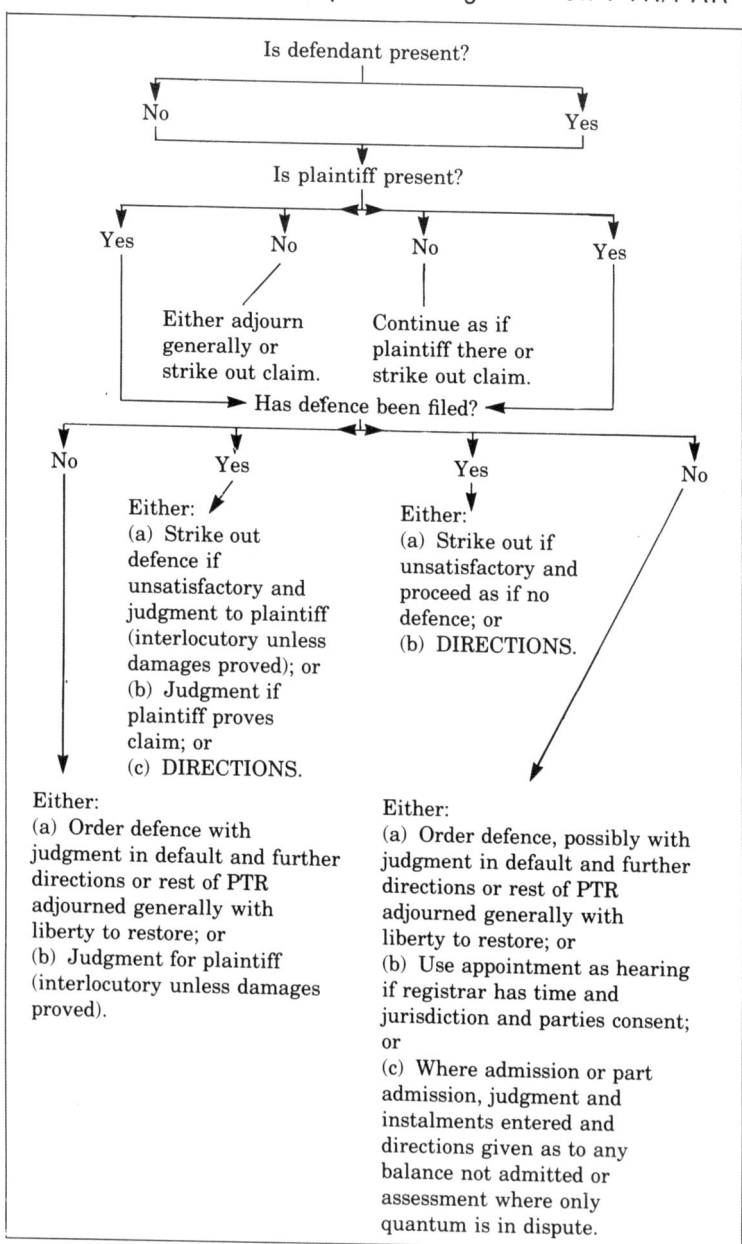

Is defendant present?

No — Yes

Is plaintiff present?

Yes — No — No — Yes

Either adjourn generally or strike out claim.

Continue as if plaintiff there or strike out claim.

Has defence been filed?

No — Yes — Yes — No

Either:
(a) Strike out defence if unsatisfactory and judgment to plaintiff (interlocutory unless damages proved); or
(b) Judgment if plaintiff proves claim; or
(c) DIRECTIONS.

Either:
(a) Strike out if unsatisfactory and proceed as if no defence; or
(b) DIRECTIONS.

Either:
(a) Order defence with judgment in default and further directions or rest of PTR adjourned generally with liberty to restore; or
(b) Judgment for plaintiff (interlocutory unless damages proved).

Either:
(a) Order defence, possibly with judgment in default and further directions or rest of PTR adjourned generally with liberty to restore; or
(b) Use appointment as hearing if registrar has time and jurisdiction and parties consent; or
(c) Where admission or part admission, judgment and instalments entered and directions given as to any balance not admitted or assessment where only quantum is in dispute.

better particulars, a copy of the draft pleading or the request must be produced to the registrar. The registrar can, of his/her own motion, order specified further and better particulars but s/he cannot order a party to amend.

(7) Where liability is admitted but quantum is in dispute, the registrar can enter judgment and give directions as to assessment of damages.

(8) Where there is an admission, judgment can be entered for the amount admitted and directions given as to any balance. Execution can be stayed but not where the dispute concerns a dishonoured cheque and there is a pending counterclaim unless there is fraud or a total failure of consideration.

(9) Where the case is ready to be set down for hearing the parties should try to give a realistic time estimate. The number of witnesses to be called is particularly relevant.

(10) The registrar may exercise any of his interlocutory powers at the review (see Chapter 6).

7.2   Third party proceedings

Where a defendant to an action claims against any person not already a party connected with the subject matter of the action, s/he must proceed by way of a third party notice (N 15) (Ord 12).

7.2.1   Requirements   In a default action prior to a hearing or pre-trial review (PTR) date being fixed the following is required:

- A third party notice (N 15) and copies for the plaintiff and third party. No leave is required.
- A self-addressed envelope (if by post) or bailiff's fee (see Table of Fees).

In a default action after a hearing or pre-trial review date is fixed or in a fixed date action the requirements are as follows:

- An application for leave to issue plus a copy for plaintiff.
- A third party notice plus copy for service.
- A self-addressed envelope (if by post).

7.2.2   Points to note

(1) If leave to issue a third party notice is requested and granted on a PTR the registrar will often adjourn the PTR so that directions in both the main and third party proceedings can be made together.

(2) Although the third party has 14 days in which to file a defence, judgment in default cannot be obtained other than at the hearing of the action if he does not attend (Ord 12, rr 2 and 3(3)).

(3) In some cases (especially road accident cases) it may be appropriate for the plaintiff to bring in the third party as a second defendant.

CHAPTER 8

TRANSFERS

8.1 To another county court

Transfers to another county court occur where a judge or registrar considers that the case could be more conveniently dealt with by another court (Ord 16, r 1) or where proceedings were started in the wrong court (see 1.2.12). However, the court may alternatively order that the matter continues in the present court or strike it out (Ord 16, r 2).

Transfer may be on the court's own motion or on an application with at least two days' notice (Ord 16, r 4(i)). The defendant may apply ex parte for the case to be transferred to his/her home court. The views of the plaintiff are normally sought in such a case (Ord 16, r 4(2)).

8.2 To the High Court

Transfers to the High Court are undertaken by order of the High Court if that court 'thinks it desirable', or by the county court either of its own motion or by an application (Ord 16, r 9) on one of the following grounds (CCA 1984, s 42):

- An important question of law or fact.
- A claim or counterclaim likely to exceed jurisdiction.
- A counterclaim or set off and counterclaim involves matters beyond jurisdiction.

A notice of transfer (N 278) is given by the court to all parties and the court transfers all the papers (cf from High Court 8.3 below). A judgment sum for more than £2,000 may be transferred to the High Court for enforcement (CCA 1984, s 106) (see also 13.1).

8.3 From the High Court

Under the CCA 1984, s 40 transfer is undertaken either:

- Where the parties consent.
- Where the case is within county court jurisdiction; or
- Where the High Court considers no important question of law or

fact will arise and the case is deemed suitable for determination by the county court.

The party having carriage of the action must lodge all appropriate papers (see *Practice Direction* (1988) 25 March) at the High Court which sends them to the county court. In addition upon transfer the county court fixes a PTR (N 273). However, if the directions have already been made in the High Court, the court may set the matter down for hearing (Ord 16, r 6(1) as amended by the CC (Amendment) Rules 1989, r 8).

CHAPTER 9

ARBITRATIONS

The two main types of arbitration heard in the county court are those heard by a registrar under the 'small claims' procedure and those heard by external arbitrators.

9.1 'Small claims' procedure

Any proceedings in which the claim does not involve more than £500 are automatically referred for hearing by a registrar. At present authority is divided as to whether this rule applies where the counter-claim exceeds £500. The 'no-costs' rule applies here (see 9.2.3 and 15.5) and an application may be made for reference to a judge or outside arbitrator.

However, a reference to arbitration may be rescinded on application where:

- A difficult question of law or complex facts are involved.
- An issue of fraud arises (the consent of the party charged is required).
- There is an agreement of the parties to try the dispute in open court.
- It would be unreasonable to proceed to arbitration because of the subject matter (eg injunction), the parties' circumstances, or if the interests of the other parties are likely to be affected (Ord 19, r 2(4)).

9.2 Outside arbitration

Under Ord 19, r 2(1), (5) non-automatic reference may be made in cases over £500 on application by party or by consent. Unlike the 'small claims' procedure the 'no costs' rule (see 9.2.3 and 15.5) does not apply and while any party may apply for an application to be referred to a judge no referral to arbitration by judge is granted without the leave of a judge. Similarly, there is no referral to an outside arbitrator without both parties' consent. It should be noted that once there has been a reference to arbitration in a non-automatic case other matters within the court's jurisdiction may also be referred to arbitration including a counterclaim exceeding £500 (cf 9.1 in small claims cases).

9.2.1 Directions and terms The registrar will make directions either at a pre-arbitration review or, at some courts, automatically (see Sample form 2 on p 72).

9.2.2 The hearing The most important provision in the hearing is that the normal rules of evidence do not apply so that proceedings are informal and in chambers. Although the arbitrator can adopt any procedure considered convenient, an inquisitorial approach is encouraged and cross-examination by the parties must be allowed (*Chilton* v *Saga Holidays plc* (1986) 1 All ER 841).

The arbitrator may adjourn the hearing to enable an expert's report to be obtained or to view the subject matter of the complaint. The decision is normally given orally but may be in writing and is entered as a judgment.

9.2.3 Costs In arbitration proceedings which have been referred the only costs recoverable are costs on the summons, costs of enforcing the award and any witnesses' expenses. (Ord 38, r 13). Party and party solicitor's costs are not recoverable (see 15.2) in these cases but the arbitrator may award further costs incurred by unreasonable conduct on the part of the opposite party.

9.2.4 Setting aside the award Awards can usually be set aside only for an error of law on the face of the award or for misconduct by the arbitrator. The requirements for setting aside are as follows:

- A fee of £10.
- A notice of application (containing grounds) must be submitted to the judge plus copies for service.
- A notice must be served within 14 days after judgment is entered (Ord 37, r 7).

However, if an award is given in the absence of a party, that party can apply to an arbitrator to set aside the award and order a new hearing (Ord 37, r 2).

CHAPTER 10

HEARINGS

10.1 General information

10.1.1 Actions All matters are heard before a judge except the following, which are heard before a registrar:

- Any action or matter in which the defendant fails to appear or admits the claim.
- Any action or matter in which the amount involved does not exceed £1,000.
- Mortgage possession claims.
- Interlocutory matters.
- Injunctions, but only where the registrar has the power to try the matter and in any event not interim injunctions (Ord 13, r 6(2)).
- Interim delivery-up (Ord 13, r 7(i)(*d*)).
- Hire purchase and consumer credit cases but not where the action is defended and the amount involved exceeds £1,000.
- Local authority possession cases where the judge has given leave (usually only if undefended).
- Summary proceedings for possession where the judge has given leave (Ord 24, r 5(2)).
- Enforcement proceedings other than committal.
- Assessment of damages not exceeding £1,000 unless the defendant fails to appear or the action has the consent of the parties and leave of the judge (Ord 22, r 6(2)).
- Certain applications under the Married Women's Property Act 1882, Matrimonial Homes Act 1983, Children Act 1975 and the Inheritance (Provision for Family and Dependants) Act 1975.
- Any other action or matter with the leave of the judge and consent of the parties (Ord 21, r 5(*a*)).

10.1.2 Rights of audience Under the CCA 1984, s 60 rights of audience can be granted to the following:

- Any party.
- A barrister or solicitor.
- A solicitor/agent.
- Any other person with leave of the court.

In addition in local authority possession and rent cases, any authorised person may address the court on behalf of the local authority.

Companies, however, must appear by solicitor or counsel unless the court authorises otherwise (CCA 1984, s 60(1)(*g*)), but a party may have limited assistance from a friend in court (*McKenzie* v *McKenzie* (1970) 3 A11 ER 1034).

10.2 Evidence

Generally, witnesses must give evidence orally under examination in open court (Ord 20, r 4). There are, however, other means to present evidence.

10.2.1 Affidavits Affidavit evidence may be given in chambers unless otherwise ordered or rules otherwise provide (Ord 20, r 5), but the court can order affidavit evidence to be used in open court (Ord 20, rr 6 and 8). Any party desiring to use affidavit evidence at a hearing must serve notice of the intention to do so together with a copy of the affidavit on the other party at least 14 days before the hearing. The other party has up to seven days before the hearing to object (Ord 20, r 7(1)). However, in a fixed date action where no defence is filed, affidavit evidence is admissible without notice (Ord 20, r 7(2)).

10.2.2 Witness summons Under Ord 20, r 12 witness summonses (N 20) may be issued to compel both oral evidence and the production of documents. The requirements upon issue are:

- request (N 286);
- plaint Note;
- conduct money if served by court;
- self-addressed envelope, if by post;
- notice of hearing date.

It should be noted that conduct money must be sufficient to cover travelling expenses both ways as well as compensation for loss of time (£16 for a police officer and £8.50 for anyone else). Also, remember to inform the witness of any adjourned hearing date and where leave is required, to issue the witness summons within seven days of the hearing date. A summons must be served personally not less than four days before a hearing (CC (Amendment) Rules 1989, r 9 amending Ord 20, r 12).

10.2.3 Expert evidence Unless all parties agree and leave of the court is given, no expert evidence (including medical evidence) may be adduced at a trial or hearing (Ord 20, rr 27 and 28).

10.2.4 Hearsay Hearsay evidence is not generally admissible except where allowed by the Civil Evidence Act 1968 (see Ord 20, rr 14–24).

10.2.5 Requirements in certain undefended proceedings The following is a list of the documents and evidence required from the plaintiff in certain types of uncontested cases:

Local Authority Housing Act cases

- Evidence from the housing officer; and
- a copy notice of seeking possession.

Rent and Housing Act possession cases

- A tenancy agreement; and
- a copy notice to quit (where appropriate) and proof of service.

Specific delivery and Consumer Credit Act orders

- An affidavit in support exhibiting agreement; and
- any notice of termination.

Mortgage Possession

- An affidavit;
- an original charge certificate or deed; and
- a Matrimonial Homes Act search (priority period not having expired prior to commencement of proceedings).

CHAPTER 11

JUDGMENTS AND ORDERS

11.1 Default judgments

11.1.1 In default of defence Where no response is filed in default actions or where there is an unqualified admission the plaintiff may apply for judgment in default (see also 5.2).

11.1.2 Failing to obey direction Where a direction has been made which includes a striking out or debarring order with leave to enter judgment in default under Ord 22, r 5 no further application or notice is required to obtain judgment.

11.2 Summary judgments

Under Ord 9, r 14 summary judgment may be applied for where it is alleged there is no defence and where the claim is for £500 or more. The requirements on issue are:

- Notice of application plus copy for service.
- Affidavit in support plus copy for service.

The notice and affidavit must be served on the defendant at least seven days before the return date and the affidavit in support must:

- verify facts relied upon; and
- state that there is no defence to all or part of the claim notwithstanding any 'defence' filed.

Although a simple form of affidavit is sometimes used, in all but the simplest cases it might be more appropriate for a more detailed affidavit in support, especially where the facts are not straightforward.

At the hearing of the application the registrar needs merely to be satisfied that there is a prima facie defence no matter how weak it may appear, in order to grant leave to defend. Such leave may be unconditional or subject to such conditions as the registrar considers appropriate including, for example, payment into court of all or part of the sum claimed to abide the event.

11.3 Judgments generally

11.3.1 Basic procedure Under Ord 22 judgments and orders are drawn up and served by the court (Ord 22, r 1(2)). Where there is an order for payment of money, the time limit is usually specified, failing which the time period is fourteen days from the date of judgment (Ord 22, r 2(1)). Where taxation takes place, costs are payable fourteen days after taxation unless otherwise ordered (Ord 22, r 2(2)) and the court may order instalment payments or suspend payment altogether (CCA 1984, s 71).

11.3.2 Recovery of land Generally, an order for possession must not be postponed to a date later than 14 days from judgment. There are, however, exceptions:

(1) Rent Acts and Housing Acts. Under the Rent Act 1977 and the Housing Act 1980 (subject to qualifications) possession can only be ordered 'if reasonable'. In such cases a discretionary period of 14 days to six weeks may be allowed unless it is a mandatory case under the Housing Act 1988 when possession must be ordered within 14 days.

(2) Mortgage possession actions. An order for possession must be for a minimum of 28 days (for suspension of a mortgage possession action see 11.4.3).

(3) Forfeiture of lease. A possession order for non-payment of rent has a minimum of 28 days.

(4) Summary possession procedure. Under Ord 24 if an occupation was originally unlawful then the court will usually order 'possession forthwith'.

11.3.3 Injunctions Under the provisions of Ord 29, injunctions:

- must usually be served personally (Ord 29, r 1 (2));
- must fix a time limit (Ord 22, r 3); and
- are enforceable by committal (Ord 29, r 1(1) also see 13.14.2).

11.3.4 Specific delivery/return Specific delivery/return is usually ordered with a fixed period of between 14 to 28 days from service of the order. Return is usually suspended on payment of the value of the goods or any unpaid balance together with judgment for the arrears and costs, all of which can be ordered to be paid by instalments.

11.3.5 Certificates of judgment Copies or duplicates of a judgment or order are supplied by the court on receipt of a written request which must state the reason why a certificate is required (eg the enforcement of debt in the High Court or proof of debt in bankruptcy proceedings).

11.3.6 Registration of judgments Every judgment (over £10 or more including costs) is registered if not satisfied within one month from the date of judgment. The judgment remains on the register for a period of six years. Searches are made at Registry Trust Ltd, 173–175 Cleveland Street, London W1P 5PE (Tel (01) 380 0133).

11.3.7 Interest on debt or damages Interest from the date the cause of action arose until judgment must be claimed in particulars of claim to be recoverable on judgment (Ord 6, r 1a) (see 2.5.2). An application to add it later may not automatically succeed (see *Ward v Chief Constable of Avon and Somerset* (1985) *The Times*, 17 July).

Interest on damages for personal injuries or deaths which exceed £200 must be given by the court unless the court considers there are special reasons to the contrary.

Court interest (as opposed to statutory or contractual interest) runs from the date the cause of action arose until judgment or prior payment but not beyond. The current rate of court interest is 15 per cent per annum.

11.3.8 Setting aside judgment Where both parties were present or represented at the original hearing, the only basis on which a rehearing (as opposed to an appeal) can be ordered is where new evidence is available which could not have been produced at the previous hearing (Ord 37, r 1(1), (N 372)). The requirements for setting aside judgment are as follows:

- Notice of application plus copy for service issued within 14 days of judgment.
- Seven clear days' notice to the other side.

Any judgment or order made in the absence of one of the parties may be set aside on an application on notice (Ord 37, r 2). The court may attach conditions to the setting aside such as payment into court of a sum of money to abide the event and/or payment of the opposition's costs of the application and costs thrown away.

11.4   Suspension and variation of judgments and orders

11.4.1   Judgment or order for money   Applications to suspend or vary payment of a judgment or order for money can be made under Ord 22, r 10 (N 245). The requirements on application by a judgment debtor are:

- An application plus two copies; and
- a self-addressed envelope, if by post.

An ex parte application can be made by a judgment creditor for a variation order to pay by instalments rather than by a lump sum or smaller instalments (Ord 22, r 10(2)). The requirements are:

- An application (N 294)
- a plaint note; and
- a self-addressed envelope, if by post.

If application is made by a judgment creditor on notice for larger instalments or earlier payment (Ord 22, r 10(3)), the requirements are:

- An application plus two copies;
- a plaint note; and
- a self-addressed envelope, if by post.

11.4.2   Warrants of execution   Under CCA 1984, s 88 warrants of execution may be suspended on application on notice. The court may impose conditions as to costs before suspension (Ord 25, r 8) (see 13.3.3).

11.4.3   Possession of land   Applications to suspend or stay the order or warrant are made to the registrar (Ord 25, r 8). The authority to suspend is derived from the particular statute giving jurisdiction to make the original order. For example:

(1) In applications under Ord 24 where trespassers take possession of land there is no power to suspend the order. However, where original entry was lawful it is possible to suspend the order under Ord 24, r 7 but in any event not for longer than six weeks (Housing Act 1980, s 89).

(2) Mortgage possession applications. The Administration of Justice Act 1970, s 36(2) (*b*)(iii) gives the court the power to suspend the

order if arrears can be paid off within a reasonable time. This varies from registrar to registrar and may be for a period of up to about three years, although a stay of two years is most common. However, the registrar may suspend the warrant for a short period to enable a sale or re-mortgage of the property to be effected.

(3) Tenancies. The court has a wide discretion to suspend orders on protected or statutory tenancies in the private sector (other than cases in Part II, Schedule 15 to the Rent Act 1977); secure tenancies (other than cases in Part II, Schedule 2 of the Housing Act 1985); assured tenancies (other than 'mandatory' cases) and assured shorthold tenancies under the Housing Act 1988.

(4) Non-protected tenants. In cases in Part II, Schedule 15 of the Rent Act 1977, Part II, Schedule 2 of the Housing Act 1985, and 'mandatory' cases under the Housing Act 1988, s 89 of the Housing Act 1980 applies and no suspension longer than six weeks from the original order can be made.

In addition, it appears that a warrant can only be suspended after it has been executed if the original judgment is set aside. An application to suspend a warrant does not automatically have the effect of staying the warrant pending hearing of the application (see *Moore* v *Lambeth County Court Registrar* [1969] 1 WLR 141 and Ord 37, r 8(2)).

Where there are persistent unmeritorious applications to suspend the warrant of execution or to set judgment aside, or where the applicant persistently fails to attend on the applications, the court has no power to refuse a further application without leave but can impose a condition that no further application can be made unless the costs thrown away on previous applications are paid first (*Thames Investment and Securities plc* v *Benjamin* [1984] 1 WLR 1381).

(5) Relief from forfeiture. Under s 138(1)–(10) of the CCA 1984 where there are rent arrears, a minimum of 28 days must be given and can be extended before possession is recovered. If the arrears and costs are not paid before possession the lessee has six months after possession to pay them to obtain relief (s 138(9A)). Relief may be granted by the court where grounds other than arrears of rent are claimed.

CHAPTER 12

PAYMENT INTO AND OUT OF COURT

12.1 Requirements

Money may be paid into court at any time before judgment. The provisions are outlined in Ord 11 and the requirements are:

- the summons or sufficient information to identify the action (ie the plaint number);
- a self-addressed envelope, if by post;
- if not payment in full, a notice identifying the nature of payment (Ord 11, r 1(1)(*b*), (2); and
- the appropriate remittance.

On receipt of the payment-in the court notifies all the parties (N 242 or N 243) (Ord 11, r 1(10)). However, notice of the payment-in will not be put with the pleadings which means that the judge or registrar will be unaware of it at the final hearing until after judgment has been given.

12.2 Effect of payment-in

Where the whole amount (including any interest claimed) is paid in, action is stayed save as to costs (Ord 11, rr 2(1), 1(8)). However, where the claim is for debt or liquidated demand and full payment including costs on summons is made within 14 days of the service of summons, action is stayed. Where payment is made outside this 14-day period or no costs are paid, then the defendant is liable to pay the plaintiff's costs up to the date the plaintiff receives the notice of payment-in. The plaintiff can either lodge a bill for taxation (where a claim exceeds £100) or ask for costs to be assessed. If these costs are not paid the plaintiff may apply for judgment for them (Ord 22, r 5(3)).

The court pays out the money in court either to the plaintiff's solicitor or to the plaintiff if acting in person. Where a lesser sum is paid into court the plaintiff has 14 days from receipt of the notice to accept it in full and final settlement, unless payment-in is made within 14 days of the service of summons in which case s/he has 21 days after the receipt of notice in which to accept. The plaintiff can then apply for his/her costs to be taxed up to the date of his/her giving notice of acceptance to the court (r 5 of the CC (Amendment) Rules 1989 amending Ord 11, rr 3(5)(*a*) and 5(2)).

A plaintiff may give notice of a late acceptance at any time before the hearing but s/he will require an order for payment-out and the court may order the plaintiff to pay the defendant's costs reasonably incurred since payment-in (Ord 11, r 5). Money paid-in pursuant to a court order 'to abide the event' is held in a deposit account until the appropriate time for payment-out. On payment-out the court must direct as to who is going to receive any accrued interest on money paid-in. If no such direction is made interest is paid to the party making the payment-in.

If a payment-in of a lesser sum is made and is not accepted by the other party and that other party, at the final hearing, recovers an amount equal to or less than the payment-in, then that party pays the other side's costs from the date of the payment-in. If they recover more than the payment-in then the other party pays all their costs. Thus, it can be seen that payment-in is an important tactical step in proceedings and must be carefully considered by both sides.

CHAPTER 13

ENFORCEMENT

13.1   General information

The main provisions governing enforcement fall under Ord 25. There are various forms of enforcement and it is for the judgment creditor ('the creditor') to decide which is the appropriate one to use.

Applications for oral examination, charging orders, attachment of earnings or a judgment summons should be dealt with by the county court appropriate to the address of the debtor or his/her place of business. The creditor will, therefore, have to ask, ex parte, for the papers to be transferred to the appropriate court for enforcement if it is not the court where judgment was obtained.

A county court judgment for £2,000 or more may be transferred to the High Court for enforcement (see 8.2).

13.2   Oral examination

Under Ord 25, r 3 'the creditor' may issue against the judgment debtor ('the debtor') or an officer of a debtor company. The person to be orally examined may also be ordered to produce any books or documents relevant to means. The requirements on issue are:

- application (N 316);
- plaint note;
- fee (see Table of Fees) and travelling expenses (optional);
- self-addressed envelope, if by post.

The oral examination is usually conducted by an officer of the court. There is no requirement that the creditor must be present. A copy of the statement of means taken either at the examination or supplied by the debtor beforehand is supplied to the creditor who may accept any proposals made therein to obviate the need for further enforcement. If the debtor fails to attend the examination the court may fix a further hearing (N 39). If the debtor fails to attend an adjourned hearing he may be liable to committal (see 13.14.1).

Although the threat of committal gives teeth to this method of enforcement the difficulty usually lies with the delay between the issue of the order and the eventual examination of a reluctant debtor. However, once an examination does take place it may yield valuable information about the debtor to enable further enforcement proceedings to be taken such as garnishee (see 13.8) and charging orders (see 13.9) or attachment of earnings (see 13.6).

13.3 Execution against goods

The main provisions for an execution against goods can be found under Ord 26. The requirements on issue are:

- request (N 323);
- plaint note;
- fee (see Table of Fees);
- self-addressed envelope, if by post.

The warrant (N 42) may issue for the whole of the unpaid balance of a money judgment and costs or for overdue and unpaid instalments exceeding at least £50 or one monthly or four weekly instalments, whichever is the greater. A warrant number will be given and this, together with the plaint number, should be used whenever directing any enquiry to the court concerning the warrant.

13.3.1 Execution against a firm Where a judgment or order is against a firm, execution may be issued against:

- the property of the firm;
- a person who admits or is adjudged to be a partner;
- any person who was served as a partner where judgment is obtained in default of defence or attendance; or
- any other person found by the registrar to be liable on application on notice by the creditor (Ord 25, r 9(3)(4)).

13.3.2 Levy The warrant is executed by bailiffs of the court for the district where the goods are situated and all enquiries concerning execution should be directed there giving the local warrant number, the plaint number and the home court warrant number.

On levy the bailiff hands a notice of levy to the debtor (N 42) or leaves the notice at the place of levy. Unless the goods have already been levied upon forcible entry is not permitted. If the goods are saleable the bailiff usually takes 'walking possession', unless payment is likely to be made in a reasonable time, in which case a period is usually allowed for payment.

Any contrary claim against the goods, eg by a spouse, must be made in writing to the bailiff (Ord 33) (see 13.3.4). There is an exemption from the levy of clothes and bedding of the debtor and his family to the sum of £100 and tools of trade up to the sum of £150. After the removal of the goods they are eventually sold at an auction and any balance after the deduction of sale fees is paid to the creditor. If there are insufficient goods on which to levy (and this is often the case) a notice to this effect is sent to the creditor or his/her solicitors who will have to consider an alternative method of enforcement.

13.3.3 Suspension of warrant Under Ord 25, r 8 a debtor may apply on notice to the court to suspend a warrant of execution giving grounds for doing so, usually a proposal for payment of the debt by instalments. The application does not of itself operate as a stay unless that is also requested. A creditor may also request suspension of a warrant. A suspended warrant may be re-issued on application by the creditor if any condition to which the suspension was subject has not been complied with.

13.3.4 Claims to goods (interpleader) Under Ord 33 a contrary claim to goods levied upon must in the first instance be given in writing to the bailiff, stating the grounds. Notice (N 358) is then sent to the creditor who has four days in which to admit or deny the claim. In the absence of a reply or where the claim is disputed, the registrar will issue an interpleader summons (N 88) for hearing on a fixed date before the judge.

13.3.5 Effectiveness Where the debt is £2,000 or more it is worth considering transferring the case to the High Court for enforcement (see 8.2). Apart from this, many warrants are returned for 'insufficient goods' or are countered by applications to suspend (see 13.3.3) or even to set aside the judgment (see 11.3.8). Sometimes they result in the debtor paying up the debt. The number of occasions when goods are actually seized and sold is smaller in comparison. Sometimes it is more effective to issue a warrant for one or more missed instalments rather than the whole of the balance.

13.4 Warrants of delivery

There are two types of warrant of delivery (Ord 26, r 16): first, that of 'specific delivery' which applies to cases where a delivery-up is ordered and second, a warrant of delivery with an alternative of paying the value of the goods. The requirements on issue are as for a warrant of execution (see 13.3).

Where, apart from delivery-up, a creditor also has a money judgment, execution for this may take place at the same time (Ord 26, r 16(4)). In hire purchase cases, where goods are already disposed of or sale costs are inadequate to meet debt, the creditor may apply on notice for the order for delivery-up to be revoked and replaced with a money judgment. Actually finding the goods, in particular where cars are involved, can sometimes be a problem, requiring the creditor to return to court for a money judgment instead.

13.5 Warrant of possession

A judgment or order for the recovery of land may be enforced by a warrant of possession (Ord 26, r 17). The requirements on issue are as follows:

* request (N 325);
* plaint note;
* fee (see Table of Fees);
* self-addressed envelope, if by post.

Where, apart from possession, a creditor also has a money judgment, execution for this may take place at the same time on paying a separate fee. The warrant lasts three months and thereafter requires leave to be extended (Ord 24, r 6(2)).

Both parties are given notice of the appointment at which the bailiff will attend at the premises. The creditor or a representative ought to be present to secure the premises after possession has been obtained by, for example, changing the locks. All persons present on the premises must leave (*R* v *Wandsworth County Court* (1975) 3 All ER 390) but note that a person in occupation who was not a party to the proceedings may apply ex parte to be joined to the proceedings (Ord 15, r 1(1)(*b*)) and for execution to be stayed, giving prima facie grounds, pending a full hearing of their application not to be evicted.

Wrongful re-entry after possession is enforceable, in the first instance, by an ex parte warrant of restitution (N 50 or N 51) and thereafter by an application for an injunction (Ord 26, r 18). For a suspension of a warrant applications are made to the registrar (see 11.4.3).

Creditors must expect a delay between the date the order for possession becomes effective and the date the bailiffs actually respond to the warrant. In the meantime debtors can, and often do, make applications to suspend the warrant, sometimes applying more than once.

13.6 Attachment of earnings

Under Ord 27 and the Attachment of Earnings Act 1971 a county court may make an attachment of earnings order to secure payments under a High Court or county court order involving a maintenance order or payments under an Administration order (see 13.12). Application is made to the court for the district in which the debtor resides (Ord 27, r 3(1)) so that a transfer may be necessary (Ord 25, r 2(1)(c)). The requirements on issue are:

• application (N 337);
• fee (see Table of Fees);
• plaint note;
• self-addressed envelope, if by post.

In addition, where judgment is of a court other than a county court:

• office copy judgment; and
• an affidavit verifying the amount due (N 321).
• If a High Court judgment, an office copy of sheriff's return (Ord 25, r 11) is required.

The name and address of the debtor's employer, if known, should also be stated in the application. In addition, the creditor may indicate on the application form that s/he wishes the court to deal with all the steps in the application in his/her absence (which is often the case).

Notice of the application (N 55) is served on the debtor with a form of reply (N 56) on which the debtor endorses details of his/her financial position. Service of the documents is usually effected by the court by post, unless otherwise provided for (eg N 58) or unless the creditor wishes to serve in which case an affidavit of service will be required.

13.6.1 Time for service and reply Notice of the application (N 55) is served on the debtor and must be effected at least 21 days before the return date or 28 days if by post. Unless the debtor pays the balance owing s/he must file the form of reply (N 56) no more than eight days from the date of service.

Where the registrar feels he has sufficient information for an attachment of earnings order to be made without the attendance of the parties' notice from the court of an intention to make an order (N 57) can be served at least 10 days before the return date. Objections to an N 57 must be made no lodged than five days from the date of service and a notice of adjourned hearing (N 58) must be served at least five days before the adjourned date.

13.6.2 Procedure For a full outline of the proceedings of issue and service of an attachment of earnings order see Diagram E.

13.6.3 The order The appropriate form is an N 60 or N 65 (maintenance) order. On considering a debtor's income and outgoings the

Diagram E: Attachment of Earnings

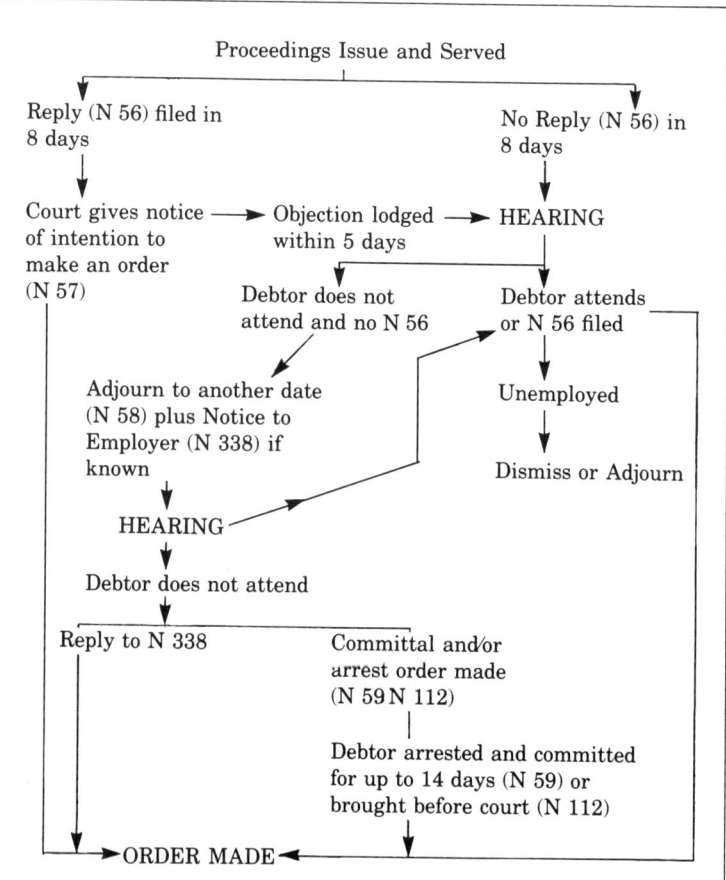

Notes:

1 N 58 must be personally served on debtor unless substituted service ordered.

2 If an employer has failed to respond to an N 338 notice the court may order the production of a Statement of Earnings (N 61) in default of which employer is liable to a fine or committal.

3 Following arrest under an N 112 the court may order the debtor to complete an N 56 and attend at an adjourned hearing at which an order can, if appropriate, be made.

registrar fixes a 'Normal Deduction Rate' (NDR) which is the amount to be deducted each week or month by the employer from a debtor's wages and a 'Protected Earnings Rate' (PER) which is the amount of the debtor's wage below which no deductions should be made. These must be specified on the form of order.

PER is usually calculated by applying allowances calculated by reference to the supplementary benefit allowances announced each year and outgoings such as rent, mortgage, rates, court orders and other significant debts. The debtor may request that the order be suspended while s/he pays the instalments ordered voluntarily. If the debtor is self-employed, the application must be dismissed. However, this does not prevent the debtor from making an instalment offer. If unemployed, the debtor's application may either be dismissed or adjourned generally with liberty to restore. At the same time a nominal instalment order can be made.

13.6.4   The employer   At any stage of the proceedings the court may send a notice (N 338) to any reported employer of the debtor requiring details of his/her earnings. The court can compel a reply (N 61). Once an attachment order is made it is sent to the employer who makes deductions and is allowed to deduct a further 50p from the debtor's earnings on each deduction for administration costs. Notice of cessation or a change of the debtor's employment must be given by the employer to the court within 10 days of the service of the order or cesser.

13.6.5   Consolidated orders   The county court makes such orders to secure the payment of a number of judgment debts. Order 27, rr 18–22 applies. An application to consolidate (N 244) two or more orders may be made by any of the parties, the employer or the court of its own motion (Ord 27, r 19). Every creditor who has an attachment order against a debtor is given notice of application and a fee is payable (see Table of Fees).

13.6.6   Discharge or cesser of order   These are made by the court where:

- the full amount of debt has been paid;
- in maintenance cases, where payments are up to date and the NDR exceeds the rate of payments or the maintenance order ceases;
- a committal order is made; (see 13.14)
- the debtor is not employed by the reported employer;
- the court is notified of another attachment of earnings order which is not to secure a judgment debt or an administration order;

- an administration order is made (see 13.12) but this can be secured by attachment order;
- a consolidated order is made; (see 13.6.5)
- a debtor becomes bankrupt; and
- a court gives leave for execution to be levied.

In addition, under Ord 13 a variation order may be applied for by any party on notice.

13.6.7 Effectiveness The pitfalls are fairly obvious particularly if the debtor is unemployed, self-employed or changes employment without notification. However the 'teeth' attached to this method of enforcement including the powers to arrest (N 112) and commit (N 59) mean that getting a response from a reluctant debtor (and employer) is not that difficult even though it may take a little time and a little persistence.

13.7 Judgment summons

This is mainly used for enforcing maintenance orders or Inland Revenue judgments. For practice and procedure see the *County Court Practice Handbook*, Chapter 23.

13.8 Garnishee proceedings

This is a procedure to seize funds being held on behalf of a debtor to go toward a judgment debt, usually from monies held in a bank, building society, or account at a solicitors' office (Ord 30). The judgment order must be for a minimum debt of £25, although there is no maximum. Application is made ex parte and the requirements on issue are:

- affidavit (N 349);
- plaint note;
- fee (see Table of Fees);
- self-addressed envelope, if by post.

If satisfied the registrar makes a garnishee order nisi (N 84), giving a return date, which is served on the parties and on the institution, etc, where it is alleged the monies are being held ('the garnishee'). Once served with the order the garnishee must pay into court such monies as it holds on behalf of the debtor to go toward the judgment debt and the costs of the application. 'Deposit-taking institutions' (eg banks and building societies) are allowed to deduct an administration fee of £30.

Notice of payment-in is sent by the court to the parties (N 350 to the judgment creditor and N 352 to the debtor). Where there are no monies in the account the garnishee gives notice to the court and the creditor and proceedings are stayed.

On the return date the registrar can order payment-out of monies received from the garnishee to the creditor. If there is a dispute the registrar will either deal with the matter or give directions. If there has been no payment-in and no negative response from the garnishee the registrar can make the order absolute.

Although useful this procedure cannot be used as a 'fishing' exercise. To get the order nisi you have to convince the court that you know of an account being held on behalf of the debtor. However, very often it turns out that the account is overdrawn.

13.9   Charging orders

This is a procedure for imposing a charge on the beneficial interest of the debtor in land or (less commonly) securities to secure payment of a judgment debt, maintenance order or order of a tribunal. A charging order will not be granted to secure an instalment order which is not in arrears.

The provisions (generally) of Ord 31 apply and the requirements on issue are:

- affidavit plus copy;
- plaint note (if county court judgment);
- fee (see Table of Fees); and
- self-addressed envelope, if by post.

Where a High Court order is to be enforced additional requirements include:

- office copy judgment;
- copy of any sheriff's return; and
- details of the balance of the judgment debt outstanding.

The contents of the affidavit (Ord 31, r 2) must give:

- debtor's name and address for service;
- details of any other known creditors;
- details of the subject matter of the intended charge; and
- grounds for the belief that the debtor has beneficial interest in the subject matter. If the asset is held by a trustee further matters need to be stated (see s 2(1)(b) of the Charging Orders Act 1979).

In the case of securities, details of the person need to be notified to protect the charge, and where interest is under a trust (eg a joint trust for sale) details of known trustees and beneficiaries must also be included. Where it is a High Court judgment details of the balance of the judgment debt outstanding are required.

13.9.1 Office copy entries Where the targeted land is registered, a request can be made by the creditor for the authority to search the registrar under s 112(3) of the Land Registration Act 1925 (N 439) and such a request is often made in the affidavit in support. Note that such a request cannot be granted unless an application for a charging order is also made.

The registrar at first considers the application ex parte and, if satisfied, makes a charging order nisi (N 86) with a return date which, together with a copy of the affidavit in support, is served on the parties, reported creditors and any person who may have a disclosed beneficial interest (eg spouse) as ordered by the court. Service of the charging order nisi is effected (usually by post) by the creditor, not the court (see r 14 of the CC (Amendment) Rules 1989) and therefore an affidavit of service is necessary. Service must be at least seven days before the hearing of return date.

On return date, depending on the circumstances, the court will either make the charging order absolute (N 87) which is served on the parties or discharge the nisi. If the creditor is not in a position to prove the debtor's beneficial interest because eg office copy entries have not been received, the court may adjourn to the first open date, ordering the nisi to continue in the meantime.

13.9.2 Protecting the charge In the case of registered property the nisi should be registered in the Land Registry as a caution and the absolute as an equitable charge. In the case of unregistered property the nisi can be registered in the Land Charges Registry as a pending action and the absolute as an equitable charge. The registrar can add the cost of registration to the costs awarded on the absolute. There is authority to suggest that a charging order cannot be registered against one of two or more beneficial owners (*Perry* v *Phoenix* [1988] 1 WLR 940).

13.9.3 Effectiveness Provided that the debtor has a valuable interest in land there is no doubt that a charging order, particularly if followed by proceedings for sale (see 13.10), is an effective method of enforcement.

13.10   Enforcement by sale

The requirements on issue in proceedings for a judicial sale (Ord 31, r 4) are:

- originating application plus copies for service;
- affidavit in support plus copies for service;
- fee (see Table of Fees); and
- self-addressed envelope, if by post.

The contents of the affidavit in support must contain:

- identification of the charging order and the property;
- the amount of charge and balance outstanding;
- verification of the debtor's title;
- identification of prior incumbrances and their amounts; and
- an estimate of the sale price.

At the hearing of the application the registrar will decide whether an order for sale should be made in which case the appropriate directions will be given (see Specimen form 3 on p 75) or whether any other appropriate order should be made for payment of the judgment debt.

Where land is owned by more than one person of whom at least one is not the debtor the charge can only be enforced by the appointment of a receiver under Ord 32 or by order for sale under s 30 of the Law of Property Act 1925.

The main drawback with enforcement by sale is where the equity in the property, after deducting all prior incumbrances, is not enough to meet the charge.

13.11   Receivers

A general power is given to the county court to appoint a receiver. The procedure is outlined in detail in Ord 32.

13.12   Administration orders

Where a debtor owes several debts which together do not exceed £5,000, the court may make an administration order which provides for payment of the total debts by single instalments which are then divided among the creditors (Ord 39). The requirements on issue for such an order are:

- request (N 92) which lists the creditors, the amount of each debt and also contains a statement of means;

- fee (see Table of Fees); and
- self-addressed envelope, if by post.

Notice of the application is sent to the creditors (N 373).

At the hearing the registrar, if satisfied that an order should be made, fixes the amount of the instalment which can be secured by an attachment of earnings order (see 13.6). The order may be reviewed, varied, suspended or revoked.

An administration order is also known as 'the poor man's bankruptcy' and is certainly useful where a debtor has several debts. From the creditors' point of view, however, it may be a long time until the debts are finally extinguished.

13.13   Enforcement of award of tribunal

The provisions for the enforcement of an award of tribunal are set out in Ord 25, r 12 and the requirements on issue are as follows:

- affidavit verifying the amount due;
- the award, order or agreement;
- fee (see Table of Fees); and
- self-addressed envelope, if by post.

Application is dealt with ex parte and can be enforced as if it were a county court judgment.

13.14   Committal

13.14.1   For non-attendance   A warrant for committal may be issued for non-attendance by the debtor at an adjourned hearing of:

- judgment summons (N 70);
- attachment of earnings (N 59);
- oral examination (Ord 25, r 3(5)).

Alternatively, the court may order the debtor to be arrested and brought before a judge (N 112). The warrant may be suspended before execution on request by the creditor or the debtor.

13.14.2   For breach of an order or undertaking   Order 29 applies and the requirements are as follows:

(1) The judgment or order must have been served (together with any appropriate penal notice) on the recipient (Ord 29, rr 1(2), (3)) or the judge must be satisfied that the recipient is aware of the order (Ord 29, r 1(6)).

(2) The order must have been served in time for it to be obeyed within the time limit allowed (Ord 29, r 1(2)(*b*)).

(3) A notice of application for committal (N 78) must be served personally unless this is dispensed with (Ord 29, r 1(4), (7), (8)) at least two clear days before the return date (Ord 13, r 1(2)).

13.14.3   Important points

(1) An undertaking given by a party in person is usually enforceable as if it were a court order (N 117).

(2) A committal order for breach must strictly follow wording of N 79.

(3) A committal order must be served on the recipient either before or at the execution of the warrant unless the judge orders otherwise (Ord 29, r 1(5)).

(4) Imprisonment is for up to two years but this can be suspended on conditions or a fine substituted or added.

(5) A person arrested under warrant is imprisoned until s/he purges contempt on a written application or the term of imprisonment expires (Ord 29, r 3).

13.14.4   Effectiveness   The effect of committal is obvious. However, it is only resorted to when all other forms of enforcement have failed and in debt claims committal does not pay the debt although the threat of it may encourage a debtor to be co-operative.

13.15   Enforcement outside England and Wales

The enforcement of county court judgments outside England and Wales (as well as outside the United Kingdom) is fully outlined in the *County Court Practice*, Order 35 and in the *County Court Practice Handbook*, Chapter 25.

CHAPTER 14

APPEALS

14.1 General

14.1.1 From registrar's interlocutory order An appeal lies to the judge and usually proceeds in chambers (unless the judge directs otherwise). Such an appeal is made to a judge on notice filed and served within five days of the order appealed against (Ord 13, r 1(10), (11)). For fee payable see the Table of Fees.

14.1.2 From registrar's final judgment or order Any party can appeal from a registrar's final order or judgment to a judge. The appeal is made to the judge on notice filed and served within 14 days of the judgment or order appealed against. For fee payable see the Table of Fees.

14.1.3 From arbitration award For information see 'Setting aside the award' (9.2.4).

14.1.4 From judge An appeal from a county court judge to the court of appeal is effected by a notice filed and served within 28 days from the drawing up of the order or judgment appealed against. In each of the above cases the time limit can be extended and execution can be stayed with leave of the court. However, there is no appeal without leave of the judge or the Court of Appeal:

- where a claim or counterclaim does not exceed half the county courts' jurisdiction in cases of contract, tort, money recoverable by statute, equity or probate;
- where the appeal is from a judge acting in an appellate capacity; and
- on questions of fact in certain housing cases (see CCA 1984, s 77(6)).

CHAPTER 15

COSTS

15.1 Generally

15.1.1 Governing rules Those that apply are Ord 38 incorporating RSC Ord 62, Pt II, rr 12, 14, 15, 16, 24, 26–28 and para 1(2) of Appendix 2; rr 8, 9, 12 and 15 of the CC (Amendment) Rules 1986.

15.1.2 Costs awards Costs are awarded on either a 'standard' or an 'indemnity' basis (see definitions at 15.2 and 15.3). If no basis is specified the standard basis applies.

The award of costs is in the discretion of the court and normally (but not necessarily) Ord 38, r 1(3) follows the event (Ord 38, r 1(2)). The court takes into account:

(1) Any offer of contribution (Ord 12, r 7).

(2) Any payment into court. A payment-in which equals or exceeds the amount awarded entitles the payer to costs from the date of payment-in (see 12.2).

(3) Any written offer to consent to the terms of a proposed order, eg an injunction unless a payment-in would have been more appropriate (Ord 38, r 1(3), Ord 62, r 9(a) of the RSC and Ord 11, r 10).

(4) Where the proposed payer is legally aided the court's discretion to award costs is limited to such amount as is considered reasonable in all the circumstances and subject to an examination as to his/her means. Often no order for costs is made against a legally aided litigant, or an order is made not to be enforced without leave of the court.

15.2 Basis of costs

15.2.1 Standard basis On this basis a reasonable amount is allowed for all costs reasonably incurred, any question of reasonableness being resolved in favour of the payer. The standard basis applies (unless otherwise ordered):

- where one party is ordered to pay the other party's costs;
- for legal aid taxation; and
- in certain cases where no specific order for costs is required (Ord 38, r 1(3), Ord 62, r 3(3), (4) and (5) of the RSC) such as an acceptance of a payment-in or on discontinuance.

15.2.2 Indemnity basis All costs are allowed unless of an unreasonable amount or unreasonably incurred, any question of unreasonableness being resolved in favour of the payee. The indemnity basis applies (unless otherwise ordered) to the:

- Costs of a trustee or personal representative (Ord 62, r 14(i) of the RSC)
- Solicitor and client bill (other than legal aid) (Ord 62, r 15(i) of the RSC)
- Costs of a party under a disability (Ord 62, r 10 of the RSC and Ord 38, r 19A).

15.3 Definition of terms

15.3.1 'Costs in the cause' Whoever wins at the conclusion of the matter gets the costs in respect of which this order was originally made (usually at an interlocutory hearing).

15.3.2 'Plaintiff's (or defendant's) costs in the cause' The party in whose favour such an order is made gets the costs of the interlocutory hearing to which it relates if that party wins at the conclusion of the matter. If they don't win they don't have to pay the other party's costs of that hearing.

15.3.3 'Plaintiff's (or defendant's) costs in any event' Whoever wins at the conclusion of the matter, the party in whose favour such an order is made gets the costs of the interlocutory hearing to which it relates.

15.3.4 'Plaintiff's (or defendant's) costs' The party in whose favour such an order is made gets the costs of the hearing to which it relates, or if it is the final hearing, the costs of the action to be taxed forthwith.

15.3.5 'Costs thrown away' The party in whose favour such an order is made is entitled to costs of that part of the proceedings rendered ineffective or set aside in respect of which the order is made eg where judgment set aside.

15.3.6 'Costs of the day' The party in whose favour such an order is made is entitled to the costs occasioned by an adjournment of a final hearing caused by the other side.

15.3.7 'Costs reserved' Whoever wins at the conclusion of the matter is entitled to the costs of the hearing at which the order was made unless the court orders otherwise. Alternatively, these costs are reserved on an interlocutory application to be considered at a later stage.

15.3.8 Bullock order A plaintiff pays the costs of the defendant against whom he fails, adds them to his own costs and recovers them from the defendant against whom he has succeeded.

15.3.9 Sanderson order An unsuccessful defendant pays the costs of a successful co-defendant directly.

15.3.10 Agreed costs There is nothing to stop the parties agreeing the amount of costs between them and orders for costs are often supplemented as in, for example: 'Plaintiffs costs on Scale 2 to be taxed if not agreed'.

15.3.11 Plaintiff's costs on claim and defendant's costs on counterclaim Where the claim and counterclaim are both successful in whole or in part, or where they both fail, and there are therefore two orders for costs, the registrar, on taxation, will treat the claim as if it stood alone and allow only such costs of the counterclaim as have been increased by it.

15.4   Scales

15.4.1 Generally Where there is a money claim the scale of costs applicable is based on a determination of the monies recovered as set out in 15.4.2 below. In non-monetary or mixed cases the scale is determined either by the trial court or the registrar on taxation, or by statute where applicable (eg Companies Acts, Insolvency Act 1986).

Sum of Money	*Scale*
Not exceeding £25	No costs unless court orders otherwise (in complex cases)
£25 – £100	Lower scale
£101 – £500	Scale 1
£501 – £3,000	Scale 2
£3,001 and over	Scale 3

15.4.2 Determination of scale The provisions of Ord 38, r 4 apply and the scale of costs is determined as follows:

(1) Plaintiff's costs—amount recovered or accepted.

(2) Defendant's costs—amount claimed.

(3) Third party's costs—amount claimed against third party.

(4) Costs payable by third party—amount recovered against third party.

(5) On counterclaim, defendant's costs—amount recovered.

(6) On counterclaim, plaintiff's costs—amount claimed.

15.4.3 Exceeding the scale The registrar on taxation has a discretion to allow items claimed both within the scale limits and in excess of them (except the block allowance). In addition, the scale can be exceeded if the court has previously so ordered although the court can also order that the scale should not be exceeded.

In exercising his discretion the taxing officer has regard to all the relevant circumstances and:

• Any complexity of the item, the issues, or the law.
• Any specialised skill or responsibility required of the solicitor and/or counsel.
• Time and effort expended by the solicitor and/or counsel.
• Amount and importance of documents involved.
• Place and circumstances of the transacted business.
• Importance of matter to client.
• Amount or value of any money or property involved.
• Any fees or allowances payable to the solicitor or counsel in respect of other items in the same case where work done in relation to those items has reduced the work necessary for the item in question (Ord 38, r 5 and Ord 62, Appendix 2, para 1(2) of the RSC).

15.5 Arbitration

Where the sum involved does not exceed £500 and the matter has been automatically referred to arbitration which has not been revoked, no solicitor's charges are allowed except:

• Fixed costs on summons.
• Costs of enforcement.
• Costs certified by the arbitrator as having been incurred by unreasonable conduct in relation to the case (Ord 19, r 6). Witness allowances and fees and proper disbursements are recoverable.

15.6 Costs and fees

15.6.1 Fixed costs for solicitors See Appendix 2 (p 101) which outlines fixed costs.

15.6.2 Assessed costs A solicitor's charges may be assessed within the amounts given in Appendix 2 on p 106. All costs awarded or payable on the Lower Scale are assessed and costs may be assessed by the court as an alternative to taxation. For further information see Appendix 2, p 106.

15.6.3 Litigants in person The rules as to the costs of litigants in person are contained in the Litigants in Person (Costs and Expenses) Act 1975. A litigant in person, if awarded costs, is entitled to:

• All disbursements actually and reasonably incurred.
• Any reasonable payments made for legal advice in connection with the case (r 15 of the CC (Amendment) Rules 1989, amending Ord 38, r 17).
• Actual loss of income involved in preparing case.
• A sum not exceeding £6.50 per hour for time spent, not involving pecuniary loss.

In the last two cases the litigant in person cannot recover more than two-thirds the amount that a solicitor might have been allowed.

15.6.4 Witness fees For a witness of fact or producing documents (including a party (Ord 38, r 13)) the maximum fee for a police officer is £16; for any other person the maximum is £22.50, unless the taxing officer considers this inadequate. Travelling and subsistence expenses may also be allowed.

For expert witnesses attending court a £22.50 minimum and £45.50 maximum (or £89.50 if Scale 3) is allowed. For qualifying to give evidence or for a written report a £22.50 maximum (or £45.50 if Scale 3) can be paid in fees. Either the trial court or the registrar on taxation may direct the maximum figure to be exceeded.

15.6.5 Certificate for counsel Unless the court otherwise orders (by granting a certificate for counsel) no counsel's fees are allowed on interlocutory applications or where there is no defence delivered and the defendant does not attend the hearing (Ord 38, r 8(1), (2)).

15.7 Taxation

15.7.1 General points

(1) Where the bill is both inter partes and legal aid it should usually be drawn on four column paper (note *Practice Direction (No 2)* (1986)), so that both taxations are dealt with together.

(2) Letters and telephone attendances are allowed on a six minute unit basis, unless there is adequate evidence that a longer period should be allowed.

(3) Where there are substantial fees for non-medical experts a full breakdown of the charges should be supplied.

(4) Copy documents will only normally be allowed if reasonably copied outside of the solicitor's office or where they are unusually (and necessarily) numerous.

(5) Only fee earner's time will be allowed for the costs of taxation, not the cost of having the bill drafted. A fee earner will not be expected to draft the bill but may claim for any necessary assistance given to the draftsman. It is therefore open to question as to whether any costs of taxation can be claimed where there is a provision taxation.

15.7.2 Quantum How much taxation there will be on costs is dependent on:

(1) What grade of fee earner should reasonably have been employed. The taxing officer will decide this on looking at the nature and detail of the case.

(2) How much time was reasonably spent by the fee earner. Solicitors must keep adequate time records and submit reasonable time estimates for perusal and preparation.

(3) The expense rate: 'The assessment of the appropriate rate per hour would be based on the taxing officer's knowledge and experience of the average solicitor or legal executive employed by the average firm in the area concerned (*Leopold Lazarus Ltd* v *Secretary of State for Trade and Industry* [1976] 12 SJ 268). Enquiry of the appropriate court would probably elicit details of the kind of expense rate being allowed.

(4) Uplift. This covers solicitors' profit, special skill or expertise, particular expedition, general supervision and the matters referred to in 15.4.3. The starting point is usually 50 per cent.

Bills for taxation must usually be lodged within three months of the order or event giving rise to the taxation. If not, leave to lodge the bill out of time may be required. The registrar has the power to disallow all or part of the bill for delay but should only do so where the delay is inordinate, inexcusable or has caused actual prejudice to the paying party.

15.7.3   Procedure for taxation inter partes   A party entitled to taxation delivers the bill plus sufficient copies for 'parties entitled to be heard on taxation' (including not only a party but any person who gives notice to the court that they have a financial interest in the taxation) as well as all necessary papers, vouchers and counsel's fee notes within three months of the order or event entitling the party to tax (Ord 38, r 20(1)).

The court sends a copy of the bill to anyone entitled to be heard with a notice (N 252) requiring him/her to say within 14 days if s/he wishes to be heard. If they do not respond to the N 252 the registrar provisionally taxes the bill and notice (N 253) is sent to the party lodging the bill giving them 14 days in which to require a full taxation. If they wish to be heard the court fixes a date for taxation on at least seven days' notice and taxation duly takes place before the registrar.

After taxation the bill and accompanying papers are returned to the party lodging them who then totals up the bill (some courts do it for them) and returns the bill to the court with the appropriate taxing fee (see Table of Fees). On receipt of the correct taxing fee and bill the court issues a certificate as to the amount and an order for payment. However, where costs are taxed on acceptance of payment-in or discontinuance a specific request for judgment in default of payment of costs must be lodged within 14 days of taxation.

15.7.4   Procedure for legal aid taxation   A party entitled to taxation delivers the bill, sufficient copies for parties, as well as all other necessary papers (see 15.7.3). Apart from these it is important that all legal aid certificates, amendments, discharges or revocations are also lodged. There can be no legal aid taxation unless there is a court order for the same or there is a discharge or revocation of the certificate. The three-month period also applies (see 15.7.2).

Among the parties 'entitled to be heard on taxation' may be the assisted person in a case where either the statutory charge applies or the assisted person has a contribution. In such a case the assisted person's solicitor should endorse the bill with a certificate to the effect that the assisted person has a financial interest in the taxation and that they have been sent a copy of the bill and informed of their right to be heard on taxation and whether or not they have indicated that they wish to be heard. If they do wish to be heard the court will fix a hearing date on at least seven days' notice before the registrar.

If the assisted person does not wish to be heard on taxation or has no financial interest in it the registrar will provisionally tax the bill (the bill is taxed on a standard basis). Thereafter the procedure is as described for inter partes bills at 15.7.3.

After payment of the taxing fee the court will issue an 'allocatur' or taxing officers' certificate showing the amount of costs to be paid by the Legal Aid Fund. In a mixed inter partes and legal aid bill this will be divided between pre-certificate costs, which are not payable by the Fund, and post-certificate inter partes and legal aid costs which are.

The assisted person's solicitor then draws up a report on case for submission to the Legal Aid Board together with the allocatur, any counsel's fee notes and a copy of the taxed bill.

Note that the registrar has the power to disallow all or part of a legal aid bill, especially if there has been delay in submitting it.

15.7.5 Taxation between solicitor and client In cases of taxation other than legal aid:

- Costs are usually taxed on an indemnity basis.
- Fourteen days' notice of taxation is given to the solicitor and the client.
- Unless otherwise ordered or the client fails to attend taxation requested by the solicitor, if more than one-fifth is disallowed the solicitor pays the costs of taxation, otherwise the client does.

15.7.6 Objections and review Under Ord 38, r 24 any party dissatisfied with taxation may apply on notice to the registrar to review the taxation within 14 days thereafter. Review of taxation of a legal aid bill cannot be requested by an assisted person's solicitor without the authority of the Legal Aid Board. The notice must specify the items in question to be reviewed and the reasons why.

The registrar may review without the attendance of the parties and gives written notice to the parties of his decision. Any party dissatisfied with the registrar's decision has 14 days in which to lodge an application to the judge for a review for which there is a fee (see Table of Fees). The notice should contain information which specifies both the items for review and the reasons for it. The judge may appoint two assessors, one of whom must be a registrar, to hear the review.

CHAPTER 16

SPECIFIC STATUTORY JURISDICTIONS

16.1 Solicitors Act 1974

(1) No action can be brought by a solicitor to recover costs in either a contentious or non-contentious matter until the expiration of one month from the delivery of the bill (s 69(1) and (2) of the 1974 Act).

(2) Unless the costs have been taxed, no action can be brought by a solicitor to recover costs in a non-contentious matter unless the solicitor has previously informed the client in writing of his/her right to require the solicitor to obtain a certificate of remuneration from the Law Society and of the statutory provisions relating to the taxation of costs (Solicitors Remuneration Order 1972, Part 3).

(3) The client can ask the court on originating application for a taxation of the bill either within one or 12 months of its delivery if, in the latter case, no action has otherwise been taken in relation to the bill.

(4) A solicitor may either issue an ordinary default summons or apply for taxation on an originating application under s 74 of the 1974 Act. If in reply to a default summons the defendant challenges the amount of the bill the court can also order taxation.

(5) The solicitor has 14 days from the date of the order to lodge his bill for taxation (Ord 38, rr 21(6), 20(1)).

(6) Taxation is on an indemnity basis (see 15.7.5 above).

16.2 Family matters

The county court also has 'family' jurisdiction including matrimonial matters under the Matrimonial Causes Act 1973, the Married Women's Property Act 1882 s 17; estate disputes under the Inheritance (Provision for Family and Dependants) Act 1975 and the Matrimonial Homes Act 1983. In addition there is jurisdiction to deal with adoption, custodianship etc. For details of these matters reference should be made to other books in this series. There are, however, one or two matters that should be highlighted.

16.2.1 The Law of Property Act 1925, s 30 This provision enables an originating application to be made to the court to determine the beneficial interest of a party in property and for orders in relation thereto. It is particularly applicable to co-habitees.

16.2.2 The Domestic Violence and Matrimonial Proceedings Act 1976 This enables parties to a marriage or co-habitees to apply for non-molestation and/or ouster orders affecting themselves and any children. The procedure is as laid down in above, except that powers of arrest can also be obtained.

16.3 Tenancies

16.3.1 Residential tenancies These are fully dealt with in *Residential Tenancies* (1988) by Richard Colbey, published by Longman. It should be noted, however that the Housing Act 1988 introduces new forms of tenancy such as the 'assured tenancy' (similar to the existing 'protected tenancy') and the 'assured shorthold tenancy'. The latter restricts the tenant's security and grounds for possession are divided between 'mandatory' grounds where the court must grant possession and 'discretionary grounds'.

Enfranchisement under the Leasehold Reform Act 1967 is commenced by originating application. For details as to procedure see the *County Court Practice Handbook*, p 189.

16.3.2 Business tenancies The provisions of Order 43 apply here. The county court has jurisdiction under Part II of the Landlord and Tenant Act 1954 which deals with security of tenure and Part I of the Landlord and Tenant Act 1927 which deals with compensation for improvements. Part II deals with convenants not to assign or make improvements without consent.

Financial jurisdiction (under Part II of the 1954 Act) which does not exceed £5,000 is 'nav'. However, this can be exceeded by agreement between the parties (s 63(3) 1954 Act). For venue see 2.1.7 above. However, the rule as to venue (Ord 4, r 8) is widely interpreted following *Sharma* v *Night* (1986) 1 WLR 757.

The requirements on issue of an originating application for a new tenancy under Part II of the 1954 Act are:

• originating application (N 397) and a copy for each respondent;

- form of request;
- appropriate fee (see Table of Fees).

The procedure is as follows:

- Court fixes return date.
- Summons must be served within two months of issue unless extended (Ord 43, r 6(3)).
- Respondent must file an answer in 14 days.
- PTR at which directions given (see Sample form 4 on p 78).
- Final hearing.

It is important to note that the time limits set down by the Landlord and Tenant Act 1954 within which proceedings must be issued must be strictly observed. In addition although an application for interim rent can be made (s 24A of the Landlord & Tenant Act 1954) it is often adjourned to the main hearing. If there is a preliminary issue eg whether a time limit has been breached, the registrar will usually order this issue to be tried first.

Applications to exclude the provision of the 1954 Act (s 38(4) of the 1954 Act) are made jointly and are usually dealt with without a hearing. The originating application must state inter alia grounds for the application and the 'nav' (see 16.4.2 above) of the property or consent to jurisdiction. Both parties should be separately legally represented and the order should be provided by the parties in form N 404(1) together with a copy of the lease containing the clause excluding the Act. The application is usually dealt with by the registrar without requiring the parties to attend.

CHAPTER 17

FURTHER READING

17.1 Standard Works

The County Court Practice (Butterworths)
This is published annually and is the 'bible' of the county court containing all the relevant rules, statutes, forms and fees as well as useful procedural tables and notes.

The Rules of the Supreme Court (Sweet and Maxwell)
The equivalent of the *County Court Practice* as used in the High Court which contains much material of use and application in the county court.

The County Court Practice Handbook Ninth edn (Longman) 1989, by Robert Blackford.
A full guide to county court practice with over 300 subject headings designed for the legal practitioner.

County Court Practice and Pleadings (Butterworths)
A summary of the law and practice accompanied by useful precedents for pleadings.

Longman Litigation Practice
A looseleaf encyclopaedia covering all aspects of civil litigation.

17.2 Longman Books

The following are books from the Practice Notes series which deal with specific matters of reference to the county court and which are recommended for further detailed study of the topics covered:

Residential Tenancies (1988) by Richard Colby

Consumer Law (1988) by P Walker

Contentious Costs (1988) by P Rigby

Personal Injury (1988) by N Saunders.

Detailed studies of relevant topics designed with the legal practitioner in mind include:

Evidence: Law and Practice (1987) by Eric Cowsill and John Clegg

Injunctions (1987) by David Bean

Recovery of Money (1989) by John Gatenby

Service of Documents by Tony Radevsky.

SAMPLE FORMS

Sample form 1: Pre-Trial Review Directions

In the BRENTFORD COUNTY COURT Case No: _____

Between _____ Plaintiff

and _____ Defendant

Registrar's Notes:

Upon hearing Plaintiff(s) Letter/Counsel/In person/Solicitor/No appearance/Rep. and Defendant(s) Letter/Counsel/In person/Solicitor/No appearance/Rep.

IT IS ORDERED that:

1. Defence Struck Out/the Defendant do, within _____ days of (today) (service of this order) file in the Court Office a fully itemised defence, if any, to the Plaintiff's claim, and deliver a copy to the Plaintiff, and that if he fails to do so, be debarred from defending altogether, and the Plantiff be at liberty to enter Judgment under Order 22, Rule 5, County Court Rules 1981.

2. The Plaintiff/Defendant do, within _____ days of _____, file in the Court Office further and better particulars of his claim/defence/counterclaim as specified in the Plaintiff's/Defendant's request dated the day of _____ and deliver a copy to the Plaintiff/Defendant.

3. The Plaintiff do, within _____ days of today, file in the Court Office a reply and defence, if any, to the Defendant's counterclaim, and deliver a copy to the Defendant, and that if he fails to do so be debarred from defending the counterclaim filed herein and the Defendant be at liberty to enter Judgment on the counterclaim.

4.   The Plaintiff/Defendant/both parties do within _____ days of today/close of pleadings file in the Court Office and deliver to the other party a list of what documents are or have been in their possession or power relating to the dispute or disputes in these proceedings/limited to special damage.

5.   Either party shall have the right—within 7 days of receiving such list of documents to request copies of any of the documents so listed by the other party and that upon receiving such request the other party shall supply photo-copies of the documents so requested within 7 days of receiving such request.

6.   That the amount of the Plaintiff's claim or Defendant's counter-claim be agreed if possible, subject to liability.

7.   Expert(s) and/or Medical reports to be exchanged within _____ days thereafter/from the date of this Order/at least from the date of trial and agreed if possible and in default of agreement expert evidence to be limited to _____ witness(es) and _____ medical witness(es) for each party and limited to those witnesses whose reports have been disclosed.

8.   Relevant photographs and sketch plans, if required, to be agreed if possible and if not the parties shall provide them at the hearing.

9.   The Pre-trial review be adjourned/generally with liberty to restore/until

10.   (a) The action be set down for hearing on
     (b) The action be set down for hearing upon the filing of certificates of readiness by either party/both parties together with estimate of time.
     (The Court must be *immediately notified* of any change in a time estimate.)

11.   Liberty to apply.

12.   The costs of this Pre-trial review be costs in the cause.

Dated this: _____   Registrar: _____

Sample form 2: Pre-Arbitration Review Directions

In the BRENTFORD COUNTY COURT   Case No: _____

Between   _____   Plaintiff(s)

and   _____   Defendant(s)

Upon hearing Plaintiff(s) Letter/Counsel/In person/Solicitor/No appearance/Rep. and Defendant(s) Letter/Counsel/In person/ solicitor/No appearance/Rep.

IT IS ORDERED that these proceedings be referred to the arbitration of the REGISTRAR OF THE COURT/   (whose award shall be entered as the Judgment in this action on the following terms UNLESS OTHERWISE DIRECTED

1. Any hearing shall be informal and the strict rules of evidence shall not apply.

2. At the hearing the Arbitrator may adopt any method of procedure which he may consider to be convenient and to afford a fair and equal opportunity for every party to present their case.

3. If any party does not appear at the Arbitration, the Arbitrator may make an award on hearing any other party to the proceedings who may be present.

4. Where an award has been given in the absence of a party, the arbitrator shall have power, on that party's application, to set the award aside and to order a fresh hearing, as if the award was a judgment and the application was made pursuant to the appropriate County Court Rule.

5. With the consent of the parties and at any time before giving his decision and either before or after the hearing, the Arbitrator may consult any expert or call for an expert report on any matter in dispute or invite an expert to attend the hearing as an Assessor.

6. Subject to the provisions of the County Court Rules in respect of claims involving £500 or less, the costs of the action up to and including the entry of judgment shall be in the discretion of the Arbitrator to be exercised in the same manner at the discretion of the Court under the appropriate provisions contained in the County Court Rules.

IT IS FURTHER ORDERED

1. The Plaintiff shall within _____ days from today fully particularise his claim in detail.

2. The Defendant shall within _____ days from today give full details of his defence to each claim and/or allegation made by the Plaintiff.

3. Each party shall within _____ days from the date (of service) of this Order send to the other party and lodge with the Court a copy of every document upon which they wish to rely at the hearing and shall not be permitted to produce at the hearing any document not so served without leave of the Court.

4. If any party proposes to produce and use an expert's report (including estimates and/or bills for repair) a copy of that report is to be sent to the other party and the Court not less than fourteen days before the date of the arbitration hearing. Such report should be agreed if possible.
(NB The cost of an expert's report and/or the expert's necessary attendance at the arbitration hearing may be recoverable from the unsuccessful party).

5. Any relevant sketch plans and photographs (of the place of the accident) to be agreed if possible and if not the plaintiff shall provide them at the hearing.

6. Special damage to be agreed if possible (ie Actual pecuniary expense).

7. General liberty to apply for further directions if necessary.

8. Costs (if any) in the cause—(Only applicable if the claim or counterclaim exceeds £500).

THE ARBITRATION WILL BE HEARD AT BRENTFORD COUNTY COURT _____ ON THE FIRST OPEN DATE AFTER _____ THAT IS THE _____ DAY OF _____ AT _____ AM/PM ESTIMATED TO LAST _____, OR ON A DATE TO BE FIXED ON APPLICATION BY EITHER PARTY WHO MUST CERTIFY THAT THEY ARE READY AND GIVE A REALISTIC TIME ESTIMATE.

Dated this _____ day of _____ 19_____

Address all communications to the Chief Clerk, Brentford County Court, Alexandra Road, Brentford, Middlesex. TW8 0JJ
Court Office usually open Monday to Friday only 10 am to 4 pm)

REGISTRAR

Sample form 3: Precedent Directions on Order for Sale (Ord 31, r 4)

In the BRENTFORD COUNTY COURT   Case No: _____

MR REGISTRAR
   the _____ day of _____ 19____

Between   _____   Plaintiff

and   _____   Defendant

UPON THE APPLICATION of the Plaintiff by Originating Summons
AND UPON HEARING the Solicitors for the Plaintiff
AND UPON READING the documents on the Court file recorded as read AND IT APPEARING that the Plaintiff is by virtue of the Charging Order specified the First Schedule hereto entitled to an equitable charge upon the interest of the Defendant in the property specified in the Second Schedule hereto

IT IS ORDERED

1. that the costs of the Plaintiff of this application be assessed in Chambers and paid by the Defendant.

2. that (unless within (28) days of this order the Defendant redeems the said charge and pays the said costs) the said property be sold without further reference to the Court at a price of not less than £ _____ (save that the sale price or reserve be fixed by the Court).

3. that pursuant to Section 90 of the Law of Property Act 1925 and for the purposes of enabling the Plaintiff to carry out the sale, there be created and vested in the Plaintiff a legal term of 3,000 years in the said property as if the said charge had been created by deed by way of legal mortgage pursuant to the said Act.

[3. that pursuant to Section 90 of the Law of Property Act 1925 and for the purpose of enabling the Plaintiff to carry out the sale of the said property, there be created and vested in the Plaintiff a legal term of years for the remainder of the term granted by the lease under which such property is held by the Defendant less the last day thereof.]

4. that the following Account and Inquiries be taken and made that is to say:
   (*i*) An account of what is due to the Plaintiff
   (a) under and by virtue of the said Charging Order; and
   (b) for his said costs
   (*ii*) An Inquiry as to what interest the Defendant has in the said property
   (*iii*) An Inquiry whether there are any, and if any, what other liens charges incumbrances upon the said property or upon any, and if any, what part/parts thereof respectively, and what are their priorities and what is due on account thereof respectively.

5. that the Defendant do within (14) days after personal service upon him of this order file at the Court Office—ALEXANDRA ROAD, BRENTFORD, MIDDLESEX—an affidavit stating what (if any) deeds and other documents relating to the title of the said property are in his possession or power, and whether any deeds or other documents relating to the said title are known by him to be in the possession or power of any other person or persons, and if so, stating name and address of every such person, and that they do within the same time lodge at the Court Office all (if any) such deeds and documents as are stated by him to be in his own possession or power.

6. that the Defendant do within (28 days after personal service upon him of this order) (within 14 days of exchange of contracts pursuant to this order) deliver to the Plaintiff possession of the said property.

7. that unless otherwise agreed by the parties interested therein, the proceeds of sale of the said property after payment thereout of (a) what shall be due to any incumbrancers other than the Plaintiff and (b) all proper costs charges and expenses incurred in connection with the said sale, be lodged in court to the credit of this application:

$$A \qquad B$$
$$v$$
$$C \qquad D$$

19 Proceeds of sale of Freehold/Leasehold property subject to further order.

8. that the parties are at liberty to apply for possession and generally.

9. that upon the Defendant redeeming the said Charge and paying the Plaintiff's costs of obtaining and executing this Order (including what is due to auctioneers and solicitors), this Order shall cease to have any further effect, but without prejudice to the validity of any contract made prior to or without notice of such redemption and payment.

THE FIRST SCHEDULE

The Order dated _____ of the _____ made in the Application

THE SECOND SCHEDULE

The _____ hold property known as _____ (and registered at Her Majesty's Land Registry under Title Number _____)

Sample form 4: Directions for Pre-Trial Review – Application for New Tenancy

In the BRENTFORD COUNTY COURT Case No: _____

Between   _____   Applicant

and   _____   Respondent

Upon hearing _____ for the Applicant and _____ for the Respondent and considering a communication from the _____

IT IS ORDERED THAT:

1. The Respondent(s) Application for interim rent be heard with the Originating Application.

2. The Respondent do file and Answer within _____ days (t)hereafter.

3. The following matter be tried as a Preliminary Issue namely (as raised in Paragraph No _____ of the Respondent's Answer).

4. Report(s) by Valuers or Surveyors be agreed if possible and that,

if not, such expert evidence be limited to _____ witnesses for each party such reports to (be limited to the Preliminary Issue) (include Lists of Comparables) (and) be exchanged within _____ days (t)hereafter.

5. The Applicant and the Respondent do within _____ days (t)hereafter file and deliver lists of documents relating to the matters in this Originating Application (limited to the Preliminary Issue).

6. There be inspection of documents within _____ days of the delivery of lists.

7. The costs hereof be costs of the (Applicant) (Respondent) (in cause) (reserved).

The HEARING of this (Originating Application) (Pre-Trial Review) be (adjourned generally with liberty to restore) and set down for a date to be fixed upon (either) (all parties) filing Certificates of Readiness for trial.

The HEARING of the Preliminary Issue be (Adjourned generally with liberty to restore) and set down for a date to be fixed upon (either) (all parties) filing Certificate(s) of Readiness for trial.

On the _____ day of _____ 198_____ at _____ O'clock

Dated _____

The Court Office: Alexandra Road,
Brentford, Middlesex
TW8 0JJ

FEES AND COSTS

County Court Fees Order 1982 (SI No 1706)

[As amended 1983, 1984, 1985 and 1986]

Schedule 1: Fees

1. The fee payable on entering a plaint or any other originating process includes:
   (a) the examination and filing of the application, petition, request or other process or any amendment to it;
   (b) the preparation and issue of any summons or other originating document and of any second or subsequent successive summons or origination document together with any notice of hearing;
   (c) except where Fee No 2 applies, the service by the court of the summons, application, petition or request and any notice of hearing;
   (d) the examination and filing of any affidavit in support of or in opposition to application;
   (e) the issue of an interlocutory application except where a fee is specifically prescribed;
   (f) except where otherwise provided, the trial or hearing of any action, originating application, petition or appeal and of any interlocutory application in the course of the proceeding together with the drawing, entering, sealing and issue of the judgment, order or certificate given or made thereon, and the service of the judgment, order or certificate by post.
2. Where any claim, counterclaim, originating application, notice of application or petition is amended and the fees paid before amendment are less than those which would have been payable if the document as amended had been so drawn in the first instance, the party amending the document shall pay the difference.
3. Fee No 1 (ii) shall not be payable on an originating application for the taxation of a solicitor's bill of costs.
4. Where value added tax is chargeable in respect of the provision of any service for which a fee is prescribed by this Schedule, there shall be payable in addition to that fee the amount of the value

added tax.

5. In relation to an action for the recovery of goods under a hire-purchase agreement 'value' in this Schedule means the unpaid balance of the total price at the date of the issue of the relevant process.

Col 1 *No and description of fee*	*Col 2* *Amount of fee*	*Col 3* *Method of charging fee*
1. COMMENCEMENT OF PROCEEDINGS (*i*) On entering a plaint for the recovery of a sum of money or the delivery of goods. Where the sum claimed or the value of the goods—		1. (i) Where a sum of money is claimed as an alternative to a claim for another sum of money or to the delivery of goods this fee is to be calculated on the greater sum of money or the value of the goods, whichever is the greater.
does not exceed £300	10p for every £1 or part thereof claimed. Minimum fee £7	Where a sum of money is claimed (whether by way of interest or otherwise) in addition to another sum of money or to the delivery of goods then for the purpose of calculating this fee the additional sum is to be added to the sum on which this fee would otherwise be calculated.
Exceeds £300 but does not exceed £500	£37	
Exceeds £500 or is not limited to a particular amount	£43	

On a claim for delivery of goods it shall be the duty of the plaintiff to estimate the value of the goods and the amount so estimated shall be entered in the request. If the value appears subsequently to the court to have been underestimated, the plaintiff shall pay the difference between

Col 1 *No and description of fee*	Col 2 *Amount of fee*	Col 3 *Method of charging fee*
		the amount paid by him on entering the plaint and the fee which would have been payable if the estimate had been correct.
(ii) On the commence-ment of proceedings for any other remedy or relief (other than an order freeing a child for adoption or an adoption order) whether by plaint, originating application, notice of application, petition, appeal or otherwise	£30	1. (ii) Where such a claim is joined with a claim for a sum of money then this fee or Fee No 1 (i) calculated on the sum of money claimed is payable whichever is the greater.
		Where two or more such claims are joined in the same proceed-ings the maximum fee payable is £40. On delivery of a counterclaim which ex-ceeds the amount of the claim there shall be paid the amount by which the fee calcu-lated on the amount of the counterclaim ex-ceeds the fee paid by the plaintiff or applicant.

2. SERVICE

On request for service by bailiff of any docu-ment except—
(a) an order in Form N 69;
(b) an interpleader summons under an execution;
(c) an originating appli-cation for an adop-tion order;

Col 1 *No and description of fee*	Col 2 *Amount of fee*	Col 3 *Method of charging fee*
(d) an order made under s 23 of the Attachment of Earnings Act 1971; (e) an order made under Ord 25, r 3(4);	£5	Fee No 2 is payable in respect of each person to be served, but in respect of a document not requiring personal service only one fee is payable in respect of two or more persons to be served at the same address. This fee is not payable where service is to be effected by post pursuant to Ord 7, r 10(2).
2A APPEALS ETC (i) On giving notice of an appeal to the judge from the registrar (ii) On an application to the judge to set aside the award of an arbitrator	£10 £10	
3. TAXATION (i) On the taxation of costs of expenses	For every £1 or part thereof allowed, 5p	3. (i) No fee is payable where costs are allowed without taxation pursuant to Ord 38, r 18 or 19.

Note—The Lord Chancellor has directed (1) that in any case where a party has been awarded a proportion only of his costs, this fee should be calculated on the amount allowed on taxation as the party's costs in the action or matter, and not on the proportion of those costs which he is entitled to recover from the other party: (2) that where the costs of an assisted person fall to be taxed between party and party and between solicitor and client, the taxing fee attributable to purely solicitor and client items should be the difference between the taxing fee payable on the party and party items of the bill and the taxing fee payable on the total of the bill: it should be noted that, in view of this direction, there may be cases in which less than the minimum taxing fee will be payable.

Col 1 *No and description of fee*	Col 2 *Amount of fee*	Col 3 *Method of charging fee*
(ii) On an application to the judge to review a taxation	£10	3. (ii) The registrar may in any case before taxation require a deposit of the amount of fees which would be payable if the bill or the expenses were allowed by him at the full amount thereof. This fee is not payable if, in an action by a solicitor for costs, the judge refers the bill to the registrar under s 70 of the Act.
4. ENFORCEMENT On an application for enforcement of a judgment or order of a county court or through a county court; (i) By the issue of a warrant of delivery or of execution against goods except a warrant to enforce payment of a court fee or an order for payment of a fine...........	For every £1 or part thereof of the amount for which the warrant issues, 15p Minimum fee £5 Maximum fee £38	4. (i) On a warrant of delivery:— (a) the maximum fee is payable unless the value is stated in the judgment or in the request and in that case the fee is to be calculated on that value or the greater value if more than one. (b) where a sum of money is claimed in addition (whether by way of interest or otherwise), then, for the purpose of calculating this fee the sum of money is to be added to the sum on which the fee would otherwise be calculated.
(ii) By an application for an order for the attendance of a judgment debtor or any other person under Ord 25, rr 3 or 4....................	£12	

Col 1	Col 2	Col 3
No and description of fee	*Amount of fee*	*Method of charging fee*
(iii) By entering garnishee proceedings	£12	
(iv) By the issue of a warrant of possession	£25	
(v) By an application for an order charging the land or securities of a judgment debtor	£5	4. (iv) Where the recovery of a sum of money, other than this fee, is sought in addition, the appropriate fee under Fee 4 [i] is also payable.
(vi) By the issue of a judgment summons	£10	
(vii) By an application for an attachment of earnings order (other than a consolidated attachment of earnings order) to secure payment of a judgment debt	10p for every £1 or part thereof	4. (vii) This fee is payable for each defendant against whom an order is sought. Fee No 4 (vii) is not payable where an attachment of earnings order is made on the hearing of a judgment summons.
(viii) On a consolidated attachment of earnings order under Ord 27, r 18, or on an administration order made under s 112 of the Act or s 4 of the Attachment of Earnings Act 1971	Minimum fee £5 Maximum fee £40 For every £1 of the money paid into court in respect of debts due to creditors, 5p	
4A TRIBUNAL AWARDS ETC On an application for the recovery of an award under Ord 25, r 12	£10	
5. SALE (i) For removing or taking steps to remove goods to a place of deposit	The reasonable expenses thereof	5. (i) This fee to include the reasonable expenses of feeding and caring for any animals.
(ii) For advertising a sale by public auction pursuant to s 97 of the Act	The reasonable expenses thereof	

Col 1 *No and description of fee*	*Col 2* *Amount of fee*	*Col 3* *Method of charging fee*
(iii) For the appraisement of goods................	5p in the £ of the appraised value	
(iv) For the sale of goods (including advertisements, catalogues, sale and commission and delivery of goods) ...	15p in the £ on the amount realised by the sale or such other sum as the registrar may be considered to be justified in the circumstances.	
(v) Where no sale takes place by reason of an execution being withdrawn satisfied or stopped	(a) 10p in the £ on the value of the goods seized, the value to be the appraised value where the goods have been appraised or such other sum as the registrar may consider to be justified in the circumstances and in addition; (b) any sum payable under Fee 5(i), (ii) or (iii)	
6. COPIES OF DOCUMENTS For a copy of any document, or for examining a plain copy and marking it as an office copy, per page;		6. This fee is payable whether or not the copy is issued as an office copy.
(a) Typewritten.............	50p	
(b) Carbon or photographic......................	25p	
7. REGISTRY OF COUNTY COURT JUDGMENTS On a request to cancel the registration of judgment which has been satisfied..............	£1	This fee is to be paid to the county court in which satisfaction was made.

Col 1	Col 2	Col 3
No and description of fee	*Amount of fee*	*Method of charging fee*
8. ADMIRALTY ACTIONS (i) For a warrant of arrest of a ship or goods including the execution thereof or the issue of a warrant of execution where the ship or goods are not under arrest (including the execution thereof)............................	£10	
(ii) On a bail bond	£2	
(iii) On the sale of a ship or goods..................	For every £5 or part thereof of the price, 5p	
(iv) For keeping possession of a ship or goods where the registrar employs:—		
(a) a possession man	For every day, £10	
(b) a shipkeeper	The reasonable expenses of the shipkeeper employed.	

Higher Scales of Costs

CCR Ord 38, r 3(1), Appendix A

[NB—The notes running across the page are by the Registrar Editor and do not form part of the Rules.]

	Scale 1 £ 100–500	*Scale 2* £ 500–3,000	*Scale 3* £ 3,000 +

PART I

PREPARATION OF DOCUMENTS
The following items shall not apply to any action or matter to which Part II applies

1. *Institution of Proceedings:* Preparing, issuing, filing and service, of particulars of claim or originating application, petition, or request for entry of appeal to a county court, or particulars of counterclaim, or third party notice; preparing preliminary act or pleading in Admiralty action.

FOR ALL SCALES
6.50–26.50

Note 1   Except where item 14 or Note 2 below applies, no profit charges for service of any process are to be allowed.

Note 2   Where a solicitor properly makes use of a process server, the process server's charges are to be shown as a disbursement.

2. *Interlocutory proceedings:* Preparing, issuing, filing and service of any documents in connection with interlocutory proceedings, including any application or notice of application or notice of interlocutory appeal.

FOR ALL SCALES
6.50–26.50

Note 1   This item applies to an arbitration, inquiry or reference.

Note 2   Interpleader proceedings are to be treated as an application to which this item refers.

	Scale 1 £ 100–500	Scale 2 £ 500–3,000	Scale 3 £ 3,000 +

3. *Other Documents:* Preparing (including where necessary filing, serving or delivering to all parties) any document not otherwise provided for, including—
(a) any document to obtain an order for substituted service;
(b) pleadings (other than pleadings instituting proceedings), defence or counterclaim thereto, particulars of pleadings, requests for such particulars, interrogatories, affidavits and lists of documents, notice to produce, admit or inspect documents, and amendments to any documents;
(c) any other affidavit;
(d) any brief to counsel or case to counsel to advise in writing or in conference;
(e) any instructions to counsel to settle any document except where an allowance for the preparation of that document is recoverable under item 1, 2 or 3—
   first five A4 pages
   for each A4 page thereafter

FOR ALL SCALES
4.60 per page (or proportionately)
3.10 per page (or proportionately)

Note 1 Items 1, 2, and 3 include engrossing and one copy for service and are only to be allowed where the document is signed by the solicitor or his clerk duly authorised in that behalf. Any additional copies required are to be charged under item 4. Item 3(d) and (e) include copy for counsel where counsel's fee is allowed. Preparation of proofs of evidence is to be charged under item 6 and not this item.
Note 2 Item 3 is not to be allowed for

	Scale 1 £ 100–500	Scale 2 £ 500–3,000	Scale 3 £ 3,000 +

preparing a request for summons etc. or a notice of acceptance or non-accept-ance of an admission and proposal as to time of payment.

4. *copy documents:*   FOR ALL SCALES

(a) Typed top copy—
   A5 (quarto)   0.55 per page
   A4 (foolscap)   0.93 per page
   A3 (brief)   1.27 per page

(b) Photographic, printed and carbon copies—
   A5 and A4   0.19 per page
   A3   0.36 per page

Note 1 Where the construction of documents is in issue, the costs of copies supplied for the use of the judge are to be allowed.

Note 2 Copy documents required to be exhibited to an affidavit are to be charged under item 4 and the collating time is to be charged under item 6, note 2(a)(ix).

Part II

5. BLOCK ALLOWANCE

In any action for damages for per-   FOR ALL SCALES
sonal injuries, or for the cost of   11–70
repairs to collision-damaged vehicles, and in any other action or matter as the party entitled to receive the costs may elect, a block allowance shall be made in place of the items prescribed in Part I unless in any such case, the taxing officer otherwise directs.

Note 1 No profit charges for service of any process are to be allowed except (a) where item 14 applies or (b) where a solicitor properly makes use of a process server, in which case the process server's charges are to be shown as a disbursement.

	Scale 1 £ 100–500	Scale 2 £ 500–3,000	Scale 3 £ 3,000 +

Note 2 In an action (other than one relating to personal injuries or collision-damage) where a party has elected to insert a block allowance, no application may be made on taxation for an allowance in excess of the permitted maximum.

Note 3 If an action for damages for personal injuries or for collision-damage is of such unusual weight that the block allowance would be wholly inappropriate, an application should be made to the taxing officer for leave to deliver an extended bill. This application may generally be made ex parte, and before the bill is drawn, by letter setting out the grounds, although the taxing officer may require the applicant to attend him before giving his decision. The lodging of a bill in extended form will in itself be accepted as an application for leave but there is no right of election in personal injuries and collision-damage cases and, should leave be refused, no extra costs will be allowed on taxation for drawing the rejected bill. Leave will normally be granted only where it is clearly shown that there are unusual circumstances which would make the use of the block allowance wholly inappropriate or unfair.

Note 4 In cases other than for personal injuries or collision-damage the lodging of a bill which includes a block allow-

	Scale 1 £ 100–500	Scale 2 £ 500–3,000	Scale 3 £ 3,000 +

ance will generally be taken as a sufficient election. Since the taxing officer may of his own motion refuse to accept the election, with or without affording the elector the right to be heard, a preliminary application may, if so desired, be made to him ex parte by letter in any case of real doubt or difficulty.

PART III
PREPARATION FOR TRIAL

6. Instructions for trial or hearing of action or matter, whatever the mode of trial or hearing, or for the hearing of any appeal.

	Scale 1	Scale 2	Scale 3
6. Instructions for trial or hearing	such sum as is fair and reasonable not exceeding 389	such sum as is fair and reasonable not exceeding 996	Discretionary

Note 1 This item applies to an arbitration, inquiry or reference, but may only be allowed once in the same proceedings.

Note 2 This item is intended to cover—

(a) the doing of any work not otherwise provided for and which was properly done in preparing for a trial, hearing or appeal, or before a settlement of the matters in dispute, including—

(i) *The Client:* taking instruction to sue, defend, counterclaim, appeal or oppose etc attending upon and corresponding with client;

(ii) *Witnesses:* interviewing and corresponding with witnesses and potential witnesses, taking and preparing proofs of evidence and, where appropriate, arranging attendance at court, including issue of witness summons;

	Scale 1 £ 100–500	Scale 2 £ 500–3,000	Scale 3 £ 3,000 +

(iii) *Expert evidence:* obtaining and considering reports or advice from experts and plans, photographs and models; where appropriate arranging their attendance at court, including issue of witness summons.

(iv) *Inspections:* inspecting any property or place material to the proceedings;

(v) *Searches and inquiries:* making searches in the Public Record Office and elsewhere for relevant documents, searches in the Companies Registration Office and similar matters;

(vi) *Special damages:* obtaining details of special damages and making or obtaining any relevant calculations;

(vii) *Other parties:* attending upon and corresponding with other parties or their solicitors;

(viii) *Discovery:* perusing, considering or collating documents for affidavit or list of documents; attending to inspect or produce for inspection any documents required to be produced or inspected by order of the court or otherwise;

(ix) *Documents:* consideration of pleadings, affidavits, cases and instructions to and advice from counsel, any law involved and any other relevant documents, including collating;

(x) *Negotiations:* work done in connection with negotiations with a view to settlement;

	Scale 1 £ 100–500	Scale 2 £ 500–3,000	Scale 3 £ 3,000 +

(xi) *Agency:* correspondence with and attendance upon or other work done by London or other agents;

(xii) *Notices:* preparation and service of miscellaneous notices, including notices to witnesses to attend court

(b) the general care and conduct of the proceedings.

The sums sought under each sub-paragraph (*i*) to (*xii*) of paragraph (a) should be shown separately against each item followed by the total of all items under paragraph (a); the sum charged under paragraph (b) should be shown separately; and the total of the items under (a) and (b) should then follow.

Note 3 This item should be prefaced by a brief narrative indicating the issues, the status of the fee earners concerned and the expense rates claimed. The narrative should be followed by a statement in two parts —

(i) setting out the breakdown of the work done in relation to the relevant sub-paragraph of note 2(a); and

(ii) a statement in relation to care and conduct under note 2(b) referring to the relevant factors replied upon; the sum claimed for care and conduct should be expressed as a separate monetary amount as well as a percentage of the work figure.

Note 4 Telephone calls will be allowed as a time charge if, but only if, they stand in the

	Scale 1 £ 100–500	Scale 2 £ 500–3,000	Scale 3 £ 3,000 +

place of an attendance whereby material progress has been made and the time has been recorded or can otherwise be established. A notional conversion into a time charge of letters and routine telephone calls will not be accepted.

Routine letters and telephone calls to the court office, counsels, and counsel's clerk can be separately charged for and do not form part of item 6(b): *Foot* v *London Borough of Wandsworth* [1987] 6 CL 307 (CC).

Note 5 Where an action is settled before delivery of the brief, the costs of all work reasonably and properly (but not prematurely) done are allowable, and the taxing officer, having regard to the circumstances of each case, must decide whether the work was reasonable and proper and that the time for doing it had arrived.

Note to Parts III, IV and VI. Where in the opinion of the taxing officer, it would have been reasonable to employ a solicitor carrying on business nearer to any relevant place, he shall not allow under Parts III, IV and VI more than he would have allowed to such a solicitor.

PART IV
ATTENDANCES

7. *Lodging:* To lodge papers, when proceedings transferred to county court, including preparation of all necessary documents.

| | 6.50 | 6.50 | 11.00 |

8. *Counsel:* Attending counsel in conference including attending to appoint the conference, for each half hour or part thereof.

FOR ALL SCALES
11.00

	Scale 1 £ 100–500	Scale 2 £ 500–3,000	Scale 3 £ 3,000 +
9. *Interlocutory attendances etc:* Attending at court, or in chambers, on an interlocutory or any other application to judge or registrar in the course of or relating to the proceedings including time travelling thereto —			
(a) without counsel	not exceeding 29	not exceeding 80	not exceeding 99
(b) with counsel	6.50–14	6.50–21	6.50–27.50

> *Note* 1 This item applies to further consideration pursuant to Order 23, rule 3.
> *Note* 2 This item applies to an arbitration, inquiry or reference.
> *Note* 3 Interpleader proceedings are to be treated as an application to which this item refers.

10. *Examination:* On examination of witness under Order 25, rule 3, or RSC Order 26, rule 5, as applied by Order 14, rule 11, for each half-hour or part thereof.

FOR ALL SCALES
3.50–10.50

> *Note.* This item is allowable where any responsible representative of the solicitor attends.

11. *Trial or hearing:* Attending the trial or hearing, or hearing of an appeal from an interlocutory or final order or judgment, or to hear a deferred judgment, or where trial is adjourned for want of time or on payment of costs of the day, including time travelling thereto per day or part of a day

time travelling thereto per day or part of a day	not exceeding	not exceeding	not exceeding
(a) without counsel	49	118	171
(b) with counsel	6.50–16	6.50–58.50	6.50–85

	Scale 1	Scale 2	Scale 3
	£	£	£
	100–500	500–3,000	3,000 +

Note 1 An attendance on the examination of a witness under Order 20, rule 13, is to be treated as an attendance to which this item relates.

Note 2 This item applies to an arbitration, inquiry or reference. If the reference or inquiry was directed at the trial and began on the same day, this item is only to be allowed once in respect of that day.

Note to Part IV: Attendances in court or at chambers or on counsel in conference should appear with a note of the time engaged.

PART V
COUNSEL'S FEES

	Scale 1	Scale 2	Scale 3
12. (a) With brief on trial or on hearing	28–100	34.50–231	Discretionary
(b) Where the trial or hearing is continued after the first day or is adjourned for want of time, or on payment of costs of the day or on examination of witness under Order 20, rule 13, for each day or part of a day	14–51.50	17.50–116	Discretionary
(c) With brief on further consideration pursuant to Order 23, rule 3, or to hear a deferred judgment; with brief on application in the course of or relating to proceedings: with brief on examination of witness under Order 25, rule 3, or RSC Order 26, rule 5, as applied by Order 14, rule 11; with brief on hearing or judgment summons	10.50–41	13–57	15–79.50

	Scale 1 £ 100–500	*Scale 2* £ 500–3,000	*Scale 3* £ 3,000 +

(d) Where there is no local Bar in the court town or within 25 miles thereof, if in the opinion of the registrar the maximum fee allowable with the brief is insufficient, a further fee may be allowed, not exceeding for each day on which the trial or hearing takes place

FOR ALL SCALES
20

Note 1 For the purpose of this sub-item there shall be deemed to be a local Bar only in such places as may from time to time be specified in a certificate of the General Council of the Bar published in their Annual Statement.

The General Council of the Bar has certified that the following towns have a Local Bar. viz.:—Birmingham, Bournemouth, Bradford, Brighton, Bristol, Cambridge, Cardiff, Chester, Chichester, Colchester, Exeter, Guildford, Hull, Ipswich, Leeds, Leicester, Liverpool, Manchester, Middlesbrough, Newcastle-upon-Tyne, Newport, Norwich, Northampton, Nottingham, Plymouth, Preston, Sheffield, Southampton, Swansea.

If counsel has more than one brief on the same day in the same court, that is not a fact to be taken into consideration: *Isaacs* v *Isaacs* [1955] P 333. [1955] 2 All ER 811.

Note 2 This sub-item is not allowed in any court within 25 miles of Charing Cross.

	Scale 1	Scale 2	Scale 3
(e) On conference in chambers or elsewhere: for each half-hour or part thereof	6.50	10.50	15.00
and for leading counsel:	7.50	18.00	28.00
(f) For settling any document including particulars of claim, defence, interrogatories and answer	6.50–11	11–29	13–41.50
(g) For advising in writing including advising on liability and quantum	4–12	12–34.50	14–70.50

	Scale 1 £ 100–500	Scale 2 £ 500–3,000	Scale 3 £ 3,000 +
Note 3 Fees to counsel are not to be allowed unless the payment of them is vouched by the signature of counsel or the head of chambers.			
Note 4 This item applies to an arbitration, inquiry or reference, but a fee reflecting preparation for trial is only to be allowed once in the same proceedings. If the reference or inquiry was directed at the trial and the reference or inquiry began on the same day, a fee for attending court or attending in chambers is only to be allowed once in respect of that day.			
(h) For advising in writing on liability, quantum and evidence	7.50–20	20–57	23.50– 116.50

Order 50, r 6 provides that where a pleading or other document is settled by counsel it shall be signed by him. Counsel's signature to the draft is sufficient, but counsel's name should appear on the document filed.

PART VI
TAXATION OF COSTS

13. (a) *Taxation.* Preparing bill of costs and copies and attending to lodge; attending taxation; vouching and completing bill; paying taxing fee and lodging certificate or order	7.65 20.50	7.65 57.00	7.65 73.00
(b) *Review:* Preparing and delivering objections to decision of taxing officer on taxation, or any answers to objections, including copies for service and lodging, considering opponent's objections or answers, if any; preparing for and attending hearing of review	7.65	7.65 20.50	7.65 29.50

Note: This item includes travelling time.

	Scale 1 £ 100–500	*Scale 2* £ 500–3,000	*Scale 3* £ 3,000 +

PART VII
SERVICE OUT OF THE JURISDICTION

14. Service of process out of England and Wales, to include drawing, copying, attending to swear and file all affidavits and to obtain order and the fees paid for oaths, such sum as the registrar thinks reasonable.

Fixed Costs

CCR Ord 38, r 18, Appendix B

PART I

DEFAULT AND FIXED DATE SUMMONSES AND GARNISHEE
ORDERS

Directions

1. The Tables in this Part of this Appendix show the amount to be entered on the summons (or garnishee order nisi) in respect of solicitors' charges—

(a) in an action for the recovery of a debt or liquidated demand (other than a rent action), for the purpose only of Order 11, rule 2(2) or 3(4), Order 19, rule 6, and Part II of this Appendix; or

(b) in garnishee proceedings, for the purpose only of Order 30, Rule 4; or

(c) in an action for the recovery of property, including land, with or without a claim for a sum of money, for the purpose of Part II of this Appendix or of fixing the amount which the plaintiff may receive in respect of solicitors' charges without taxation in the event of the defendant giving up possession and paying the amount claimed, if any, and costs; or

(d) in a rent action, for the purpose of Part II of this Appendix and of fixing the amount which the plaintiff may receive in respect of solicitors' charges without taxation in the event of the defendant paying the amount claimed in sufficient time to prevent the plaintiff's attendance at the hearing.

2. In addition to the amount entered in accordance with the relevant Table the appropriate court fees shall be entered on the summons.

3. In the Tables the expression 'claim' means—

(a) the sum of money claimed; or

(b) in relation to an action for the recovery of land (with or without a claim for a sum of money), a sum exceeding £600 but not exceeding £2,000;

(c) in relation to an action for the recovery of property other than money or land, the value of the property claimed or, in the case of goods supplied under a hire-purchase agreement, the unpaid balance of the total price.

4. The Tables do not apply where the summons is to be served out of England and Wales or where substituted service is ordered.

TABLES OF FIXED COSTS
TABLE 1
Where claim exceeds £25 but does not exceed £250

	Amount of charges
	£
(a) Where service is not by solicitor	21
(b) Where service is by solicitor	23.50

TABLE II
Where claim exceeds £250 but does not exceed £600

	Amount of charges
	£
(a) Where service is not by solicitor	28
(b) Where service is by solicitor	33

TABLE III
Where claim exceeds £600 but does not exceed £2,000

	Amount of charges
	£
(a) Where service is not by solicitor	47
(b) Where service is by solicitor	52

TABLE IV
Where claim exceeds £2,000

	Amount of charges
	£
(a) Where service is not by solicitor	51
(b) Where service is by solicitor	56

PART II
JUDGMENTS

Directions

Where an amount in respect of solicitors' charges has been entered on the summons under Part I of this Appendix and judgment is entered or given in the circumstances mentioned in one of the paragraphs in column 1 of the following Table, the amount to be included in the judgment in respect of the plaintiff's solicitors' charges shall, subject to Order 38, Rule 3(4), be the amount entered on the summons together with the amount shown in column 2 of the Table under the sum of money by reference to which the amount entered on the summons was fixed.

Where judgment is entered or given for a sum less than the amount claimed or for the delivery of goods of which the value or the balance of the total price is a sum less than the amount claimed, the foregoing paragraph shall, unless the court otherwise directs, have effect as if the amount entered on the summons had been fixed by reference to that sum.

Fixed Costs on Judgments

Column 1	Column 2 Sum of money		
	A Exceeding £25 but not exceeding £600	B Exceeding £600 but not exceeding £3,000	C Exceeding £3,000
(a) Where judgment is entered in a default action in default of defence..	7.50	14.00	15.50
(b) Where judgment is entered on the defendant's admission and the plaintiff's acceptance of his proposal as to mode of payment........	13.00	27.50	32.00
(c) Where judgment is entered on an admission delivered by the defendant and the court's decision is given as to the date of payment or instalments by which payment is to be made	17.50	35.00	41.50
(d) Where judgment is given in a fixed date action for— (i) recovery of a liquidated sum of money; or (ii) delivery of goods; or (iii) possession of land suspended on payment of arrears of rent, whether claimed or not, in addition to current rent. and the defendant has neither delivered a defence, admission or counterclaim, nor otherwise denied liablity..............................	26.00	39.00	48.00
(e) Where summary judgment is given under Order 9, rule 14	60.50	69.00	

PART III
MISCELLANEOUS PROCEEDINGS

The following Table shows the amount to be allowed in respect of solicitors' charges in the circumstances mentioned.

Amount to be allowed

1. For making or opposing an application in the course of or relating to the proceedings where the costs are on lower scale £8.50

2. For making or opposing an application for a rehearing or to set aside a judgment where the costs are on lower scale £8.50

3. For filing a request for the issue of a warrant of execution for a sum exceeding £25 .... £1.50

4. For service of any document required to be served personally (other than an application for an attachment of earnings order or a judgment summons unless allowed under Order 27, rule 9(1)(a), or Order 28, rule 10(2)(a)(*i*)), including copy and preparation of certificate of service £5.50

5. For substituted service, including attendances, making appointments to serve summons, preparing and attending to sweat and file affidavits and to obtain order, and the fees paid for oaths £17.00

6. For each attendance on the hearing of an application for an attachment of earnings order or a judgment summons where costs are allowed under Order 27, rule 9, or Order 28, rule 10 ...... £5.50

7. For the costs of the judgment creditor when allowed in garnishee proceedings or an application under Order 30, rule 12 ....

    (a) where the money recovered is less than £50.. one-half of the amount recovered

    (b) where the money recovered is not less than £50 .... £31.50

8. For the costs of the judgment creditor when allowed on an application for a charging order .. £31.50

9. For obtaining a certificate of judgment where costs allowed under Order 35, rule 5(3)(d) £5.25

Assessment of Costs

CCR Ord 38, r 19, Appendix C

Directions

1. The following Table shows the amount which, pursuant to Order 38, Rule 19, may be allowed where costs are to be assessed without taxation. The amount includes the fee for counsel where applicable.

2. In addition to the amount shown in the Table there may be allowed, where appropriate—

(*i*) court fees.

(*ii*) allowances to witnesses.

	Column 1 *Scale*	*Column* 2 *Amount of Charges* £
Lower Scale		39.00 to 60.50
Scale 1		43.50 to 110.00
Scale 2		68.00 to 412.50
Scale 3		99.00 to 497.00